How to be a
GENIUS

**LONDON, NEW YORK,
MELBOURNE, MUNICH, AND DELHI**

Senior editor Francesca Baines
Senior art editor Smiljka Surla

Project editor Shaila Brown
Editors Carron Brown, Steven Carton
Designers David Ball, Sheila Collins, Hoa Luc,
Marilou Prokopiou, Jacqui Swan

Managing editor Linda Esposito
Managing art editor Diane Thistlethwaite

Publishing manager Andrew Macintyre
Category publisher Laura Buller

Picture research Harriet Mills, Ria Jones
DK picture library Emma Shepherd
Production editor Maria Elia
Senior production controller Angela Graef
Jacket editor Mariza O'Keeffe
Jacket designers Yumiko Tahata, Natasha Rees

Editorial development Joanna Pocock
Design development Akiko Kato, Yumiko Tahata
Design development manager Sophia M. Tampakopoulos Turner

Puzzle advisor Joe Fullman

First published in the United States in 2009
This paperback edition published in 2013 by
DK Publishing, 375 Hudson Street, New York, New York 10014

13 14 15 16 17 10 9 8 7 6 5 4 3 2 1

Copyright © 2009 Dorling Kindersley Limited
195568 – 07/13

DK books are available at special discounts when
purchased in bulk for sales promotions, premiums,
fundraising, or educational use. For details, contact:
DK Publishing Special Markets, 375 Hudson Street,
New York, New York 10014
SpecialSales@dk.com.

A catalog record for this book is available from the Library of Congress.

ISBN: 978-1-4654-1424-3

Hi-res workflow proofed by MDP, U.K.
Printed and bound by HUNG HING, China

**Discover more at
www.dk.com**

This book is full of puzzles and activities to boost your brain power. The activities are a lot of fun, but you should always check with an adult before you do any of them, so that they know what you are doing and are happy that you are safe.

How to be a
GENIUS

Written by John Woodward

Consultants Dr. David Hardman
and Phil Chambers

Illustrated by Serge Seidlitz
and Andy Smith

CONTENTS

Emotions
Fear, anger, joy, love, and other emotions might seem like automatic mental responses, but we can use our brains to control our emotions if we want.

Automatic activity
Your brain is always active, even when you are asleep. It also keeps you alive by controlling your heartbeat, temperature, breathing, and digestion.

Perception
All of our senses are linked to our brain. When we take in the signals around us, it allows you to see, hear, touch, taste, smell, and understand the world.

YOUR AMAZING BRAIN

The brain is the most astonishing part of your body. Its billions of cells control everything you think and do, including your actions, senses, emotions, memory, and language. The more you use it, the better it works. This book is all about how to get your brain cells buzzing and, maybe, become a genius.

Perfect pair
This puzzle tests your spatial awareness—your sense of space. Which two pieces on the far right will fit together to create this hexagon shape?

B

A

C

D

E

F

Check the puzzle answers on page 186.

Thinking
Your brain is always solving problems by connecting different ideas—even when they are not part of your own experience. Only humans can do this.

A human brain is the most complex structure on Earth.

Memory
Every event or fact that grabs your attention may be stored in your memory—an amazingly efficient library of information that never runs out of space.

Language
Your brain gives you the ability to communicate and understand complex ideas using speech. You can also learn by reading words that were written long ago.

Movement
Your brain triggers and organizes your movements, so your actions are smooth and efficient. Most of this happens without you thinking about it.

Feel lost?
Life is full of puzzling problems—such as how to get to the middle of this tricky maze. It's your a-maze-ing brain that helps you find the answers.

Meet Your Brain

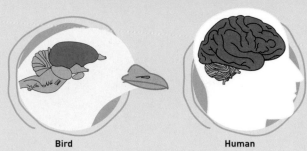

Fish **Bird** **Human**

Origin of genius
Compared to other animals, the human brain has a much bigger cerebrum (shown in orange above). This is what makes us intelligent, because we use the cerebrum for conscious thought.

MAPPING THE BRAIN

Your brain is the most complex organ in your body—a spongy pink mass made up of billions of microscopic nerve cells linked together in an electronic network. Each part has its own job, but it is the biggest part, the cerebrum, that is responsible for your thoughts and actions.

Meninges These layers cushion the brain against shock

Galen of Pergamun
A Greek surgeon named Galen of Pergamun was one of the first people to suspect that the brain was an important organ and that it controlled memories and emotions. Galen lived between 129 and 200 CE, in what is now Turkey, where he treated the gory injuries of gladiators.

Your brain is 77 percent water.

Pituitary gland
This releases chemicals called hormones into your blood. They control many functions, including growth and body development.

Hypothalamus
This is the part of your brain that regulates sleep, hunger, and body temperature.

Thalamus
The thalamus relays sensory signals from your body to your cerebrum, where they are decoded and analyzed.

Brain stem
Connected to the spinal cord, the brain stem links the rest of the body to the brain and controls heartbeat and breathing.

Skull Forms a protective casing around the brain

Cerebrum

The biggest part of the brain controls all our conscious actions and thoughts, analyzes sensory data, and stores memories.

Up to 2 pints (1 litre) of blood flows through your brain every minute.

Corpus callosum A band of nerve fibers that link the two sides of the cerebrum

Subarachnoid space This is filled with shock-absorbing fluid.

Blood supply

The brain needs a constant supply of oxygen to fuel its activities. This is delivered in the blood via the body's circulatory system of arteries, veins, and capillaries. Around one fifth of the body's entire quota of oxygenated blood is reserved for the brain.

Cerebellum
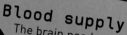
This complex folded structure helps control balance and movement.

Parietal lobe Processes information from the senses, especially from the skin, muscles, and joints

The outer brain
The cerebrum is heavily folded in order to increase the total surface area, which is packed with brain cells. It is divided into halves, the left and right hemispheres, and each consists of four lobes that have different functions.

Frontal lobe Vital to thought, personality, speech, and emotion

Temporal lobe Mostly concerned with the recognition of sound

Occipital lobe Receives nerve signals from the eyes and interprets visual information

Cerebellum

Spinal cord

The cerebrum is divided into two halves, connected by a bridge of nerve fibers. For some functions, each half is wired to the opposite side of the body, but other skills and thought processes are controlled by only one half of the brain.

LEFT BRAIN

LEFT BRAIN SKILLS
The left side of your brain is responsible for the more logical, rational aspects of your thinking, as well as your verbal skills.

Language
Your ability to express yourself in words is usually controlled by the frontal lobe of the left cerebral hemisphere.

Scientific thought
Logical scientific thinking is the job of the left side of the brain, although most science also involves being creative.

Left optic tract
Carries data from right visual field

Rational thought
Thinking and reacting in a rational way appears to be mostly a left-brain activity. It allows you to analyze a problem to find an answer.

Mathematical skills
Studies show that the left side of the brain is much better at dealing with numbers than the right side, and it is responsible for mathematical skills.

Writing skills
Like spoken language, writing skills that involve organizing ideas and expressing them in words are largely controlled by the left hemisphere.

Left visual field
Right side of each eye sees the left visual field

Two minds?
Many mental activities involve both sides of the brain, but the side that is most involved may vary. These two scans show the brain activity of two people while listening to music. The one on the left is using their right hemisphere much more, indicating a more intuitive approach, while the other person may be more analytical.

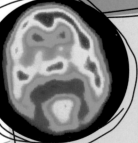

This scan shows brain activity (red areas) in the right hemisphere.

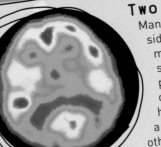

A trained musician uses the left hemisphere more.

Left visual cortex
Processes data from right visual field

RIGHT BRAIN

RIGHT BRAIN SKILLS

The right side of your brain seems to be the focus of your more creative thoughts and emotional, intuitive responses. It is also important for spatial awareness.

Optic nerve
Sends visual signals to brain

Right optic tract
Carries data from left visual field

Right visual cortex
Processes data from left visual field

Spatial skills
Your ability to visualize and work with three-dimensional shapes is strongly linked to the right side of your brain.

Art
Visual art is related to spatial skills, and the right side of your brain is probably more active when you are drawing, painting, or looking at art.

Imagination
Your creative imagination is mostly directed by the right hemisphere, although expressing that imagination involves left-brain skills.

Insight
Those moments of insight when you connect two very different ideas probably come from the right half of your brain.

Music
Like visual art, music involves a lot of right-brain activity—but trained musicians also use their left brains to master musical theory.

Crossed wires
The left side of each eye is connected to the left side of your brain, but it picks up data from the right side of your head—the right visual field. Each side of the brain processes images from the other side of the head. Each side also controls the muscles of the opposite hand.

Right-handed world
The left brain controls the right hand, and since most people are right-handed, this suggests that the left brain is usually dominant. So do left-handers use their right-brain skills more? There is no proof of this, and many left-handers have no trouble using language and logic.

TAKING SIDES

Most people are either left- or right-handed, but did you know that you can also have a dominant foot and a preferred eye? In both physical and mental tasks, the left and right sides of your brain are far from equal, and it is very rare for someone to be able to use both hands or feet equally well. Try the following tests to find which side you are on.

Eye-motion

Look straight at the nose of the girl in each of these pictures. In which one do you think she looks happier? Most people find that she looks happier in the bottom image, which shows her smiling on the left side of the picture. This is because information from your left visual field gets processed in your brain's right hemisphere, which is also dominant for interpreting emotions.

Best foot forward

The easiest way of finding which of your feet is dominant is to kick a soccer ball, but you usually take the first step of a flight of stairs with your stronger foot, too. Your preferred foot may not be on the same side as your dominant hand—you can be left-footed and right-handed or vice versa.

Try doing things with the opposite hand to normal, such as switching the hand that you hold your fork with or putting your watch on the other arm. This forces your brain to learn new ways of doing things and creates more connections between the two sides of your brain.

14

Eye see you

To discover which is your dominant eye, hold up your index finger to eye level and look past it into the distance. Then close each eye, one at a time. You will see that with your weaker eye, your finger will appear to jump, whereas with your stronger eye, it will stay in place. Your stronger eye figures out the position of things, while the weaker eye helps with depth perception.

Having one hand as strong as the other can give you an advantage in some sports. In baseball, for example, an ambidextrous hitter can switch hands to strike the ball from the best side.

Trick your brain

This exercise reveals how your brain sometimes tricks you into taking shortcuts. First, draw this upside-down picture of a face. Then turn the face the right way up and draw it again. When you compare the two pictures, you may be surprised to find that the upside-down version is the most accurate.

The left side of your brain assigns simple shapes to common objects—for example, an almond shape for an eye. So if you draw a face the right way up, you probably draw the features based on what you think they look like rather than what you see. When you look at a face upside down, however, the right side of your brain works harder to understand the unfamiliar image and you draw the shapes and lines you actually see.

Handy test

Ambidexterity is the ability to use both hands equally well. To see if you are ambidextrous try the exercise below. Take a pencil in your right hand and ask a friend to time you for 15 seconds. Starting top right, work your way along the line, putting as many dots as you can in the white circles. Then do the same on the other side with your left hand and compare the results.

Left hand start

Right hand start

You will get the farthest along the line with your dominant hand, but you may surprise yourself by just how well you did with your weaker hand. If you found that you got just as far with each hand, you are probably ambidextrous.

NERVES AND NEURONS

Your brain is connected to a nerve network that extends to every part of your body. The system is like a tree with many branches and twigs, sprouting from the spinal cord that links them to the brain. The nerves consist of bundles of cells called neurons, which also form the tissue of the brain itself.

Axon Nerve signals pass along the long axon to stimulate other neurons.

Nervous system

The small nerves that reach every corner of your body are called the peripheral (outer) nervous system. They gather data from your senses and pass it to the central nervous system—the spinal cord and brain—where it is processed. Instructions are then sent through the peripheral nervous system to your organs and muscles.

The axons of some neurons are more than 3 ft (1 m) long, making them the biggest cells in the human body.

Your brain is only three percent of your body weight, but consumes 17 percent of your body's total energy.

Branching cells

The body is made up of many different types of cells. Each is basically an envelope of fluid containing a nucleus that controls what it does. Neurons are cells with an unusual form, because they have branching filaments called dendrites that receive information from other neurons. The longest filaments, or axons, form the main nerve fibers of the body.

Cell body All the materials needed by the cell are made here.

Tingling nerves

The long axon of a neuron is like a wire that conducts electrical signals. At one end is the dendrite, which receives signals from other neurons and passes them down the cell body. These signals release chemicals that trigger more electrical impulses, which pass out and onto other neurons at the synaptic knob at the other end of the axon.

Nucleus Controls all the functions of the neuron

You could fit 30,000 neurons on the head of a pin.

Myelin sheath
This protects the long axon and speeds up nerve impulses.

Send and receive
Different neurons have their own jobs. Sensory neurons pick up signals from your senses, while motor neurons deliver signals to your muscles. Some of this activity involves conscious thought, especially if you are engaged in a skilled activity. But a lot happens automatically, controlling vital functions like your heartbeat and breathing.

Synaptic knob
The swollen end of the axon from another neuron releases chemicals that trigger nerve signals.

Nerve network
Neurons link together to pass nerve signals to one another. This activity is most intense in the brain, where around 100 billion neurons form a complex network resembling the electronic circuits of a computer. This network processes the data gathered by your senses, stores it in your memory, and gives you the ability to think.

Electrical nerve impulses shoot along the long axons of neurons at 250 mph (400 km/h).

Dendrite
Each dendrite picks up signals from other neurons.

Reflex
If you touch the sharp spine of a cactus, a pain signal shoots up a nerve in your arm to your spinal cord, which instantly triggers a nerve impulse that pulls your hand away. The impulse short-circuits the central nervous system to cause an automatic reaction called a reflex. Your brain is not involved, although it is kept informed. You move before you realize it.

Mitochondrion
Turns sugar into energy to power the cell's activities

BRAIN WAVES

Your brain is an electrical device. Simple electrical sensors can detect the tingling of brain cells as they are stimulated by other brain cells, and they show this activity on a display in the form of waves. These waves take different shapes, depending on your state of mind. Scientists can also use various types of scanners to produce images of the brain at work. These show which areas are active when dealing with different tasks.

Hans Berger

Brain waves were first recorded by German psychologist Hans Berger in 1924, using silver wires attached from the head to a device that showed the waves. He named his first recordings alpha and beta waves. Since then, scientists have recorded delta after letters of the Greek alphabet. waves, gamma waves, and theta waves.

Beta: alert

Thinking and dreaming

Different mental states generate different types of brain waves. An alert thinking state creates a fast but shallow beta wave, while a relaxed state generates a slower but deeper alpha wave. An even slower theta wave indicates drowsiness, and sleep produces a delta wave, which is slower still. The slowest, deepest delta waves indicate deep, dreamless sleep.

Alpha: relaxed

Theta: drowsy

Delta: asleep

Wernicke's area
The area of the brain that interprets language glows red here.

Medium activity
Green and yellow areas on this PET scan show sites of moderate brain activity.

Modern scanning techniques enable researchers to "see inside" the brain as it deals with different tasks. The positron emission tomography (PET) scan on the left shows a three-dimensional cutaway image of a man's brain while he is having a conversation. The areas responsible for listening and speaking appear to light up in brighter colors as they become more active.

Paul Broca

French physician Paul Broca discovered the area of the brain that controls speech. After a male patient of his who could not speak died in 1861, Broca examined his brain and found that the region now called Broca's area was damaged. Other areas of the brain have been identified in the same way.

Somatic sensory cortex
Analyzes nerve signals from the skin, muscles, and joints

Sensory association cortex
Coordinates information from all the senses

Visual association cortex
Analyzes visual data to form mental images

Wernicke's area
Interprets written and spoken language

Primary visual cortex
Receives visual data from the eyes

The cerebral cortex enables you to think and accounts for 80 percent of your brain.

Broca's area
The brain area responsible for speech is also active.

Motor cortex
Controls coordinated muscle movement

Premotor cortex
Initiates, guides, and coordinates actions

Prefrontal cortex
The main area associated with personality, thinking, and awareness

Broca's area
Controls speech and the formation of words

Auditory association cortex
Associates sound signals with memories, emotions, and other senses

Primary auditory cortex
Analyzes nerve signals from the ears

No one has discovered a part of the brain that gives a person a sense of self, or acts as the site of consciousness.

Mapping the brain

By combining modern scanning techniques with studies of brain anatomy, scientists have mapped the areas of the brain responsible for tasks such as seeing, hearing, speaking, and movement. But consciousness and learning do not seem to be related to particular areas—they may involve activity in many parts of the brain at once.

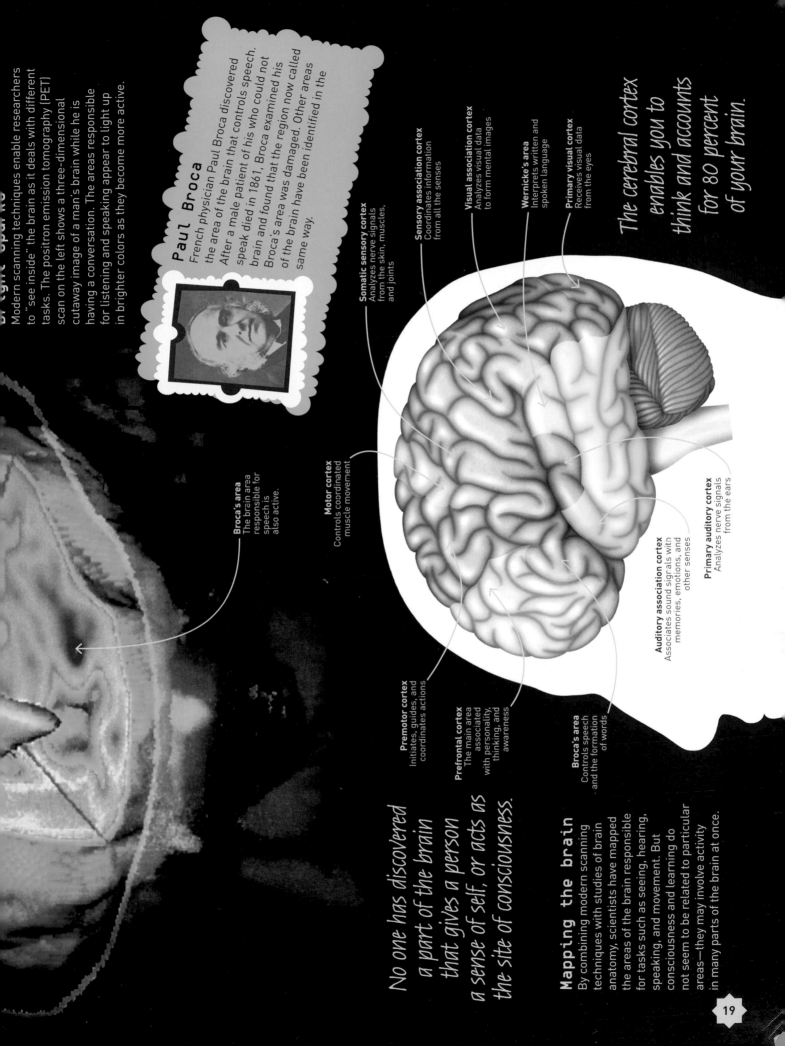

We all know what we mean by a genius, someone who is superintelligent or has amazing skills. But are these people born with these qualities or do they develop them? It turns out that while being smart is very important, a lot also depends on originality, determination, support, and hard work.

WHAT IS A GENIUS?

$$+b^2 = c^2$$

a^2

c b a

Original thinking
Italian astronomer Galileo Galilei (1564–1642) lived at a time when most people had strange ideas about how the universe worked. His genius was to study everything with fresh eyes and come up with theories based on observations and experiments. In the process, he invented modern science.

Mad scientist
Ancient Greek philosopher Pythagoras is famous for his mathematical theories. Yet he was also eccentric, remembered for forbidding his students from eating beans. Many geniuses have odd habits, usually because they are so absorbed by their work that they neglect everything else. They often become known as "mad scientists."

Geniuses' ideas are not always popular. Galileo got into serious trouble for promoting the idea that Earth was not the center of the universe.

There is a theory that it takes 10,000 hours of work to be an expert at anything—that's around ten years of practice.

Determination

Born in Poland in 1867, Marie Curie was determined to be a scientist, even though such a career was not considered suitable for a woman in the 1800s. She fought poverty and prejudice to win two Nobel Prizes for her pioneering work on radioactivily.

Child prodigy

Some people just seem to be born geniuses. Garry Kasparov was only 13 when he won the Russian junior chess championship in 1976, and he became the youngest-ever world champion in 1985. He had a natural talent, but he worked hard to make the most of it.

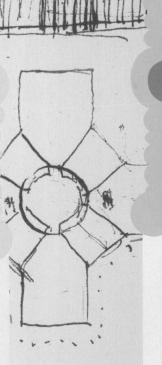

Broad view

Some geniuses do one thing extremely well, but others excel at many things. Thomas Jefferson—the main author of the U.S. Declaration of Independence in 1776—was a philosopher, archaeologist, architect, and inventor, as well as a politician who became president of the United States.

Encouragement

American sisters Venus and Serena Williams are among the greatest of all tennis players. They showed amazing talent from a young age, but they owe a lot of their success to their parents, who coached and encouraged them to build on their skills.

Come to Your
Senses

BRAIN AND
EYES

We are visual creatures. We identify most things by sight and we think mainly in visual terms. So for most of us, sight is our dominant sense. This means that a lot of the information we commit to memory is in the form of visual images. But how do the brain and eyes work together to create these images?

Image convertor

Your eye is a ball of transparent jelly lined with light-sensitive cells. Light rays enter your eye through lenses that focus an upside-down image on the cells. These cells respond by generating tiny electrical signals that pass down a bundle of nerve fibers to your brain. The cells exposed to parts of the image that are light generate bigger signals than cells exposed to dark parts, just like the pixels in a digital camera sensor. The cells turn the image into an electronic code that your brain can process.

Eye muscle One of six muscles that rotate the eye in its socket

Choroid A network of blood vessels spreads through this middle layer of the eye.

Retina The inner lining is a sheet of light-sensitive cells.

Pupil The opening in the iris allows light into the eye.

Lens The elastic lens changes shape to fine-focus the image.

Iris Muscles in the iris change the size of the central pupil.

Cornea The "window" at the front of the eye partly focuses the image.

Sclera The white of the eye forms a tough outer layer.

Reflected light Visible objects reflect light into your eyes.

Clear view
Light reflected from anything you see is focused by the cornea and lens to form a clear optical image. This is projected upside down on the back of the eye.

Automatic control
Each eye has two lenses. The cornea at the front forms one lens. Behind this is another lens made of transparent jelly, suspended by muscles that automatically change its shape to focus on close or distant objects. The colored iris controls the light entering the eye by automatically dilating (widening) or contracting the pupil at the centre.

Dilated pupil

Contracted pupil

Mental image

The cells of the retina convert light into electrical signals. These pass to the visual cortex of the brain, which turns them into an upright mental image.

Seeing in color

The cone cells in the retina respond to different strengths of basic colors such as red, green, and blue. The signals they send to the brain represent millions of dots of these colors. The brain combines the dots to create all the other colors of the spectrum, as in this simplified diagram.

Visual cortex The part of the brain that processes visual data

Optic nerve Bundle of nerve fibers linked to the sensory cells

Dark adaptation

When you turn the light off in your room at night, you can't see much. However, as the minutes tick by, you are able to see more and more. This is because the sensory cells in your eyes can adapt to the low light level—but it takes time. If you turn the light back on, you get dazzled because your eyes have adapted to the dark. They must readapt to the light, but they do this much more quickly.

Sensory cells

The image is focused on a sheet of light-sensitive cells called the retina. Some of the cells (rods) are very sensitive to dim light, while others (cones) detect color.

There are around 126 million sensory cells in each eye— 120 million rods and six million cones.

Strange effects

Bright lights and contrasting patterns can cause strange optical effects. For example, if you stare at something for a minute and then close your eyes, you see a negative afterimage. Each color is replaced by its opposite, so the yellow and red flowers shown below appear blue and cyan. This is a side effect of the way your brain processes color.

Blind spot

The point where the optic nerve leaves the eye cannot detect light, but your brain invents information to fill the gap. You can test this using the diagram above. Hold the book at arm's length, close your right eye, and focus on the cross. Slowly move the book toward you. The center of the wheel will disappear when it falls on your blind spot— but your brain will fill the gap with spokes of the wheel.

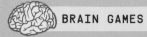
TRICKY PICTURES

The optical illusions in this gallery all play tricks on what your eyes and brain think they are seeing. They stimulate the eyes in such a way that still images seem to move, colors change, and things appear where they shouldn't.

Is it straight?

The horizontal lines in this illusion appear to be wavy, but they are all perfectly straight—use a ruler and see for yourself! Our brains interpret the lines as being wavy owing to the disjointed black-and-white lines running from top to bottom, which can also make some horizontal bands look closer than others.

Did that move?

The patterns in this picture appear to be moving, but not if you stare at any spot for a few seconds. This demonstrates what is called peripheral vision drift. Our brains perceive the colors and contrasts as moving when we are not looking directly at them, but the effect ends when we train our eyes on one spot.

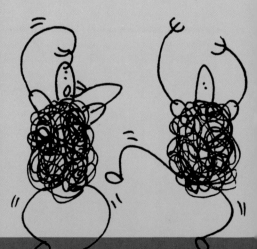

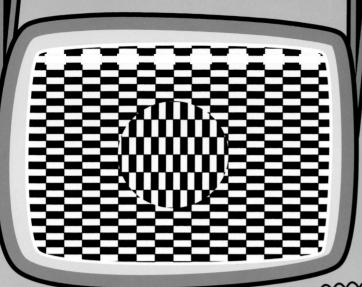

Ouch!

If you move your eyes around this pattern, called the Ouchi illusion, the circle in the middle seems to move or separate from the rectangular background, and even hovers in front of it. This illusion is not fully understood, but it probably arises from the brain being unsure of where the circle ends when you are not looking directly at it.

Jumping goldfish

Stare at the pink dot in the centre of the goldfish's head for 15 seconds and then look at the black dot in the empty bowl. You should see the goldfish in its new home. This happens because an impression of the goldfish, called an afterimage, is still left on the back of your eye.

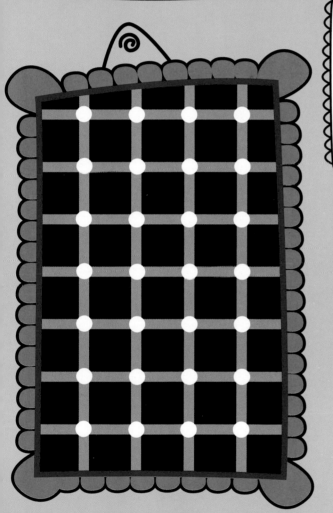

Seeing spots

This picture is called a scintillating grid because when you look at it, dark spots seem to flash (scintillate) in the intersections between the squares. The reason for this is yet to be explained, but if you tilt your head to either side, it seems to lessen the effect.

Color contrasts

Which of these green crosses is lighter? Most people would say the cross on the right. It might seem strange, but there is actually no difference between them. This illusion is known as simultaneous contrast, and it shows that the way we perceive colors is based on their surroundings.

HOW YOU SEE

Your eyes turn visual images into an electronic code that can be processed and stored in your brain. It is this mental processing that determines how you see the world. Without it, you could not make sense of all the shapes and colors. Your brain also responds to some visual effects by translating them into other types of information. This enables you to judge things like depth, shape, and distance.

Binocular vision

Each eye sees a slightly different image of the world. Try closing one eye and framing a distant object with your hands. Then open that eye and close the other. You will find that your hands are framing a different view. The images below show the different views of the same setting seen by each eye. The left eye can see the palm trees behind the boat, while the right eye sees the flowering trees. You might expect this to confuse your brain, but it combines the images to create a 3-D view.

Parallax

If you close one eye and look at a scene without moving your head, it looks flat like a picture. But if you move your head from side to side, you get an impression of depth. This is because objects that are closer to your eye seem to move more than objects that are farther away, and your brain translates the difference into a perception of depth. This parallax effect is obvious if you look out of the side window of a moving car—nearby objects like these pillars zip past, but distant objects like the trees move hardly at all.

Perspective

Another way your brain judges distance is by decoding perspective. This is the effect you get when you look up at a tall building and the walls seem to lean toward one another—even though you know they are vertical. Your brain makes an automatic calculation based on this knowledge and turns it into a perception of height.

Aerial perspective

In landscapes with long views, your brain can use another clue to assess distance. Called aerial perspective, it describes the way the color of distant objects is affected by moisture or dust in the air. It is obvious in hilly regions, as seen in this picture, where the distant hills look paler and bluer than those closer to the camera. When astronauts visited the Moon, which has no air, the absence of this effect made them think that distant hills were much closer than they actually were.

We use up to ten different ways of judging distance and depth, showing how important it is to us.

Light and shade

Objects are usually lit from above, casting shadows that vary according to their shape. Your brain uses this to judge shapes, enabling you to tell the difference between a ball and a flat disk. The reaction is so instinctive that it even works with 2-D images. These shapes look like a dent surrounded by bumps, but if you turn the page upside down, they look like a single bump surrounded by dents.

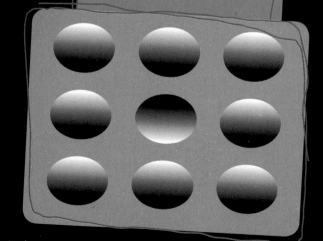

Optical illusions

Information stored in your memory helps you make sense of what you see. But it can also confuse you by applying the wrong set of rules. In this desert mirage, the blue "water" is really part of the sky. It appears in the wrong place because the view is distorted by a layer of very hot air. Since you know that it can't be the sky, you assume it is a reflection of the sky in a pool of water.

An average person can tell the difference between 200 colors, all forming part of the visible light spectrum from red to violet.

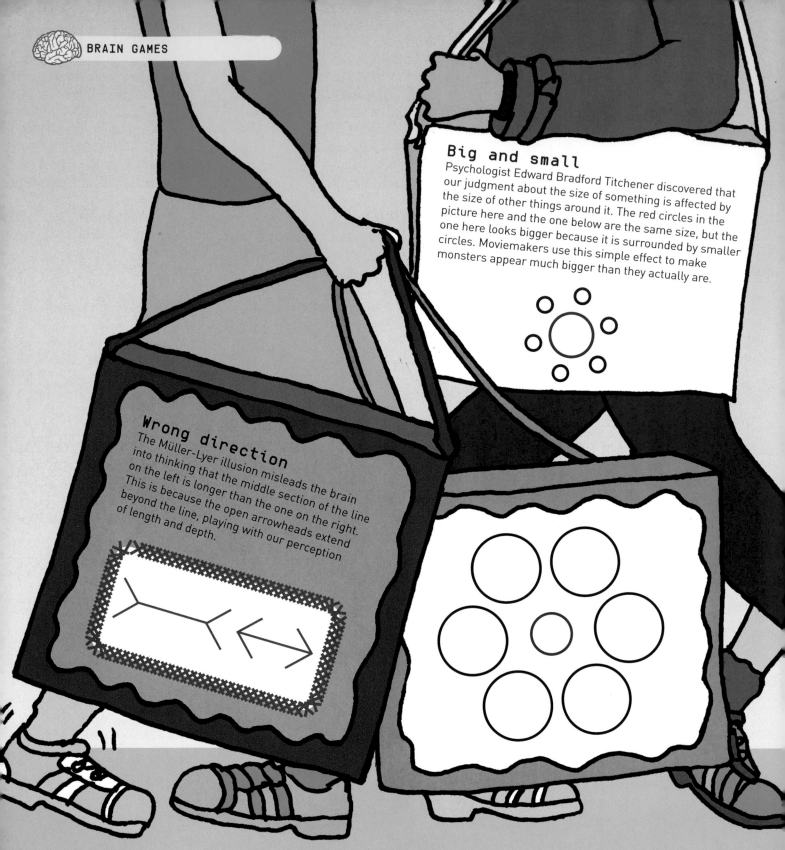

Big and small

Psychologist Edward Bradford Titchener discovered that our judgment about the size of something is affected by the size of other things around it. The red circles in the picture here and the one below are the same size, but the one here looks bigger because it is surrounded by smaller circles. Moviemakers use this simple effect to make monsters appear much bigger than they actually are.

Wrong direction

The Müller-Lyer illusion misleads the brain into thinking that the middle section of the line on the left is longer than the one on the right. This is because the open arrowheads extend beyond the line, playing with our perception of length and depth.

Some of the most effective optical illusions can be produced with simple lines and shapes. Such illusions play with our perceptions of angles, size, and shape, causing us to make unconscious assumptions about what we see. Even when we know how they work, the illusions are difficult to shake off.

SIMPLE

Is it square?

The concentric circles in this picture trick our brains into thinking that the image has depth. It also makes the perfectly straight lines of the blue square appear to bend inward.

Crossed lines

This illusion was discovered by German astrophysicist Johann Karl Friedrich Zöllner. The four parallel vertical lines appear tilted. Scientists cannot explain why we see tilted lines when they are perfectly straight!

A little bit dotty

Dots appear to join the crosses in this image, but the dots don't actually exist—they're simply gaps in the lines. Scientists disagree on an explanation. Do we see dots because the brain figures out the boundaries of shapes from little bits of information? Or do we see the illusion before the brain has processed exactly what it is we are looking at?

Two in one

This simple image contains two illusions. The black lines give a sense of perspective, stretching into the distance. This creates a second illusion in which the red line at the top appears to be longer than the one at the bottom. They are, in fact, the same size.

ILLUSIONS

The water cycle

The Dutch artist M. C. Escher was inspired by optical illusions. This picture shows a circuit of water that seems to flow impossibly uphill before tumbling down to start its journey all over again. If you look closely, you can see that the technique used is the same as that in the Penrose triangle, below.

Deathly beauty

American illustrator Charles Allan Gilbert created this famous optical illusion. What do you see in the picture? A pretty woman admiring herself in a mirror or a scary grinning skull?

IMPOSSIBLE ILLUSIONS

Look at these pictures and objects. What do you see? Is there one image or two? Is the water really flowing uphill? Illusions are not always as they seem at first glance. The brain can flip between two options as it tries to make sense of the impossible.

Face-to-face?

When the eyes and brain focus on an object, they separate it from its background, but it's not clear which is the object in this illusion.

Some people see a white vase on a black background, while others see two black people looking at each other on a white background.

Crazy cube

You can see this shape in two ways—as a small cube sitting on the inside of a bigger cube or as a single large cube with a small cube-size chunk missing from its bottom corner. This design first appeared in a floor mosaic found in the ancient Roman ruins of Pompeii, Italy.

Two or three?

Like Penrose's triangle, this object cannot be created in 3-D. You see two different perspectives at once, yet it's impossible to fit them together. Three round prongs at one end become a rectangular shape at the other. Nobody is really sure who first created this illusion—it's a puzzle from start to finish!

Tricky triangle

This illusion was created by mathematician Roger Penrose. All three straight beams of the triangle appear in front and behind one another at the same time, and they meet at right angles to one another. It would be impossible for this object to exist in 3-D.

Pressure waves

Sounds pass through the air in the form of pressure waves. You can picture these by imagining pushing one end of a long coil spring in order to squeeze the end coils together. The squeezed coils then spring apart and push against the rest of the spring, squeezing more of the coils and forming a wave of compression that passes down the spring. Sounds are transmitted through the air in the same way, as rapid vibrations squeeze air molecules together.

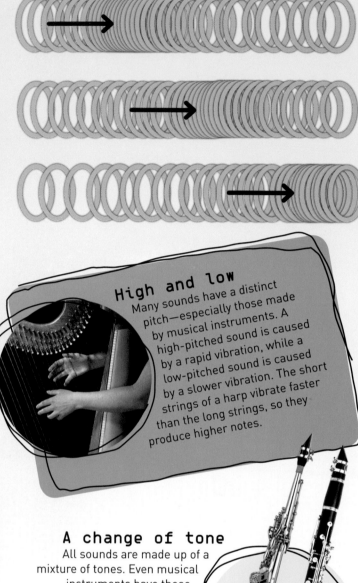

High and low

Many sounds have a distinct pitch—especially those made by musical instruments. A high-pitched sound is caused by a rapid vibration, while a low-pitched sound is caused by a slower vibration. The short strings of a harp vibrate faster than the long strings, so they produce higher notes.

A change of tone

All sounds are made up of a mixture of tones. Even musical instruments have these overtones and undertones, which give sound its character. They explain why a note played on a metal instrument like this soprano saxophone sounds so different from the same note played on a wooden clarinet.

HOW YOU HEAR

If you watch a cat prowling through long grass, you will see its ears twitching constantly as it picks up faint sounds that might betray hidden prey. We cannot twitch our ears, but we monitor sound in a similar way to keep track of the environment and avoid danger. We also use our hearing to communicate and enjoy music. Like the other senses, hearing is made possible by organs that gather data and convert it into a code that can be used by the brain. Without mental processing, sound would mean nothing.

Auricle The outer flap of the ear

Orientation

You can often locate the origin of a sound by gauging its effect on both ears. If the sound is louder in your left ear, the noise is coming from left of center. But your brain is not as good at judging the height of a sound source. If you try to locate a singing bird in a dense bush, for example, its height is harder to pinpoint than its left-right orientation.

Your ability to hear high tones diminishes as you get older, so children can hear high-pitched sounds that adults cannot.

Vibrating eardrums

Sound waves passing through the air push against your eardrums, making them vibrate. Each eardrum transmits the vibration through a series of small mobile bones to a coiled fluid-filled tube called the cochlea. The fluid in the cochlea vibrates, too, and thousands of tiny sensory hair cells in its lining convert the vibration into electrical signals that pass to the brain.

Cochlear nerve Sends nerve impulses to the brain

Semicircular canals These play an important role in balance.

Stapes Transmits vibrations to the oval window

Incus Picks up vibrations from the malleus

Skull bone

Malleus Transmits vibrations from the eardrum

Ear canal Channels sound waves to the eardrum

Eardrum Vibrates in response to sound

Oval window Transmits vibrations through to the inner ear

Eustachian tube Controls air pressure

Cochlea Turns vibrations into nerve impulses

Your ears also contain the organs that enable you to keep your balance when riding a bike.

Background noise

Your ears deliver a jumble of electronically coded noise to your brain, which sorts it out by focusing on one sound and ignoring the background noise. At a noisy party, for example, you can consciously listen to one person and ignore all the others. But you also have an unconscious tendency to ignore any sounds that are constantly part of the environment, like a whirring fan, and pay attention only to new sounds.

Lip reading

Many deaf people can understand what people are saying by reading their lips as they talk. But everyone does this up to a point. At a noisy party, it is much easier to follow what people are saying if you are watching their faces and lips. If you look away for more than a few moments, you lose track of what someone is saying.

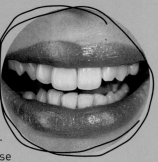

SOUNDS LIKE?

An earful!

Every day you are constantly surrounded by sounds. Tune in and see how many you can identify.

You will need:
• Pen and notebook
• Good noisy location—a supermarket or a playground, for example
• Stopwatch

Step 1

Ask your parents to take you to your chosen location. In a one-minute time period, try to write down all the things you can hear. You will be surprised by how many sounds you can identify.

Step 2

Ask your parents to make a note of what they can hear, too. Can they identify the same sounds?

🌀 **As we get older our ability to pick out sounds decreases, so your parents may have fewer sounds on their list!**

Two ears or one?

Can you hear well with one ear or do you need both ears to locate sound? Try this activity and find out.

You will need:
• Blindfold
• Selection of objects that make distinctive sounds, such as spoons, an alarm clock, a whistle, and musical instruments
• Absorbent cotton
• Friends to participate

Step 1

Blindfold a volunteer, making sure that his or her ears are not covered by the material. Then ask your other friends to stand around the blindfolded

Step 2

Give everybody but the blindfolded person an object. One at a time, ask them to make their sounds. Then ask the blindfolded volunteer to identify the sound and where it is coming from. Record how often he or she is correct.

Step 3

Now place absorbent cotton in one of the volunteer's ears to block out the sounds and repeat this activity using different noise-making objects. Record and compare the results. Was the person less successful the second time around?

🌀 **Sounds reach both ears at slightly different times, so they send slightly different signals to the brain. This information is used by the brain to detect the direction and distance of the sound.**

The three smallest bones of your body are found in your ear—the smallest is the stapes, which is around the size of a grain of rice.

Can you hear something? From whispering voices to a phone ringing, yours ears pick up all sorts of sounds. Try the following activities and find out how much information we process through our ears.

You cannot hear any sounds in space. This is because sound needs a medium to travel through, such as air or water.

What was that?

Test your hearing ability by identifying these challenging sounds.

You will need:
- Paper
- Tape
- Scissors
- Three empty bottles
- Uncooked rice
- Dried beans
- Uncooked pasta
- Empty bag
- Friends to participate

Step 1
Fill each bottle with a different material—the uncooked rice, dried beans, and uncooked pasta. Let the participants hear each shaken bottle once. Then wrap them in paper before placing them in the bag.

Step 2
Ask your volunteers to close their eyes and pick the bottles out, one by one. Can they identify what is inside the bottles by shaking them?

◎ **How good is your sense of hearing?** Throughout your life, your brain stores information it encounters, enabling you to identify the sounds you come across.

Noisy bottles

Experiment with high- and low-pitched sounds when you do this activity.

You will need:
- Three empty glass bottles
- Pitcher of water

Step 1
Fill each bottle with a different amount of water, leaving one empty. If you blow across the top of the empty bottle, it makes a low-pitched sound. If you add a little liquid and then blow, the pitch is higher—the more liquid, the higher the pitch.

Step 2
If you tap the sides of the same bottles, you get the opposite effect: the empty bottle has the highest pitch, while the fullest bottle has the lowest pitch.

◎ **There is less air when the bottle is half full, so the air vibrates faster, with higher pitch. When the bottle is empty, the vibration is slower and the pitch lower. But when you tap the bottle, it is the glass and water that are vibrating to create the sound. The greater the amount of water, the lower the pitch.**

Wolfgang Amadeus Mozart

Some people seem to have a genius for music and can play it superbly when they are very young. A few are even able to compose complex orchestral music when they are only children— something that most people would find impossible. The most celebrated of these musical geniuses is Wolfgang Amadeus Mozart, one of the greatest composers who ever lived.

Wolfgang at the age of six, performing with his sister, Nanneri, and their father, Leopold, during their first trip to Paris, France, in 1762.

Child prodigy

Born in Austria in 1756, Mozart was the son of a professional musician, so he was in the right family to learn his art. He could read music before he could read words, and began playing and composing music at the age of five. His sister was also a musician, and when Wolfgang was six, their father took them around Europe to show them off as child prodigies.

Improvising talent

Mozart was terrific at dreaming up variations on a musical theme while he was playing. According to a witness who saw him perform as a teenager, he would improvise like this for more than an hour, with such skill that even accomplished musicians were astounded. But to him this talent for fitting musical ideas together was just a party trick. The real challenge was to compose original, exciting music, which took a little longer.

Perched on a thick pillow, the young Mozart demonstrates his skill at the organ to an aristocratic audience.

In 1787, Emperor Joseph II of Austria made Mozart his court composer.

This portrait of Mozart at the age of around 26 shows his love for fine clothing.

Fun and games

Despite his musical genius, Mozart did not have a one-track mind. He enjoyed horse riding, dancing, and billiards. When he started earning serious money in Vienna, he bought a billiard table as well as a new piano. He was well known for his sense of humor, partly because he enjoyed practical jokes. He also liked showy clothes and was once decribed as appearing onstage "with his crimson pelisse and gold-laced cocked hat."

Musical memory

Mozart had an amazing musical memory. He once wrote down an entire work by another composer from memory after hearing it only twice. He was able to soak up ideas and combine them with his own in order to create music that was inventive, sophisticated, and often very powerful. Many consider it to be some of the most beautiful music ever written.

A typical small orchestra of the late 1700s accompanies a composer playing a keyboard concerto.

Hard worker

Although he had incredible natural talent, Mozart also worked very hard. He produced several drafts of each piece, adding more detail with each version until he had the whole thing completed. If he ran out of time and was going to perform the piano part himself, he would sometimes write out the parts for the other musicians and perform his own part from memory—or even make it up as he went along.

Freelance composer

In 1781, Mozart defied 18th-century convention by becoming a freelance composer and musician. At first he did well, but in 1790, he became ill. Mozart died in 1791 at the age of only 35. During his short life, he wrote more than 600 works, including symphonies, operas, and concertos for a variety of instruments.

Although he is the most famous musician of all time, Mozart was unlucky with money and died almost penniless.

TASTE AND SMELL

Your senses of taste and smell are closely connected, and they both help you enjoy your food. But your sense of smell is vital in other ways. It alerts you to danger and helps you recognize familiar places, things, and even people. Your brain reacts surprisingly strongly to smell, especially smells that you memorized long ago.

Taste bud

Most of the receptor cells that detect taste are concentrated on the tongue in clusters called taste buds. There are around 10,000 of these, each containing 50 to 100 banana-shaped cells with tiny "taste hairs" at the top. When you eat, saliva and dissolved food seep into each taste bud through a tiny pore. The cells react to chemicals in the food by sending nerve impulses to the brain.

Taste pore

Taste hair

Nerve fiber

Taste receptor cell

Simple tastes

Your taste buds can distinguish between only five taste sensations: salty, sour, sweet, bitter, and umani (savory). This combination is too limited to account for all the different tastes that you experience, and this is because your sense of smell also plays an important role in "tasting" your food. Infections such as colds and the flu can make you temporarily lose your sense of smell—and then you find that you cannot taste much either.

SALTY

SOUR

SWEET

UMANI

BITTER

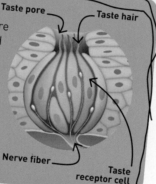

Cerebral cortex
Analyzes and relates smells and tastes

Olfactory bulb
Gathers scent signals and passes them to the brain

Olfactory receptors
Detect scent molecules in the air

Nasal chamber

Tongue

Nerve fibers
Gather data from taste buds

Scent signals

The human sense of smell is poor compared to that of many animals, but it is much more refined than your sense of taste, enabling you to detect thousands of scents. Scent molecules are carried in the air, and when you breathe in, they are detected by two patches of receptor cells located high up in your nasal cavity. Nerve fibers from these cells pass through the skull to the olfactory bulb, where more nerve cells transfer the coded scent signals to the brain.

We all have our own unique smell identity. This is determined by factors such as genes, diet, and skin type.

Instinctive reaction

The olfactory bulb is part of the limbic system at the top of the brain stem. The limbic system is an area of the brain that plays an important role in memory and emotion. This explains why scents can trigger powerful emotions and awaken dormant memories. Scent information also passes to the cortex of the brain to be analyzed consciously, but this takes a lot longer than the instinctive reaction.

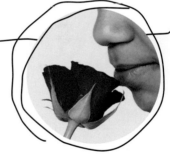

Thalamus Receives taste signals from the medulla and sends them to the cortex

Medulla Receives taste signals and relays them to the thalamus

Brain stem

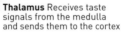

Professional senses

Some people earn a living by their noses. They include the makers of perfumes and, not so obviously, wine tasters and tea blenders. The blenders of fine teas, for example, may "taste" the teas, but their taste buds can barely identify them. They use their refined sense of smell to decide which combinations have the best flavor.

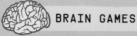

SENSITIVE SENSES

Unlike the other senses, smell and taste function by detecting chemical substances. Our sense of smell enables us to distinguish up to 10,000 different scents, and there are people who have an extra-sensitive sense of smell and taste. Try these activities and find out more about your senses of smell and taste.

In the weightless environment of space, food aromas don't often reach the nose, so astronauts miss out on a lot of food flavors.

A blocked nose

Can a blocked nose affect your sense of taste? Follow the steps below and find out.

You will need:
• Selection of foods with varying degrees of taste and flavor
• Glass of water
• Two friends

Step 1
Ask the first volunteer to sample the food, rinsing his or her mouth out with water in between tastes. Record the responses.

Step 2
Repeat Step 1 with the second volunteer, but this time ask your friend to hold his or her nose closed. Who had a better sense of taste?

When you can't smell what you are eating, it is harder to recognize food flavors. So if your nose is blocked because you have a cold, for example, food often tastes bland.

Seeing is believing!

How good are you at identifying what you are eating?

You will need:
• Selection of flavored Jell-O
• Some plates and spoons
• Blindfold
• Two friends
• Pen and paper

Step 1
Ask an adult to help you make the Jell-O. When they have set, place them on a plate.

Step 2
Put a blindfold on the first person, making sure he or she does not see the Jell-O beforehand. Then ask your friend to taste and identify th flavors. Record the results.

Smell

Try this test and find out how good your sense of smell is.

You will need:
• Blindfold
• At least six bowls and three items with strong smells such as a banana, coffee grounds, flowers, or soap
• A friend

Step 1
For each item, put two samples of it in two different bowls. Mix the bowls around.

Step 2
Blindfold your friend, and ask him or her to identify which two items smell the same. How good was your friend's sense of smell?

🌀 Our sense of smell is much more sensitive than our sense of taste—around 10,000 times more sensitive. It alerts us to danger by detecting poisonous odors and we can even identify whether food is ripe or rotten by smell alone.

Step 3
Ask the second person to identify the flavors. This volunteer should not be blindfolded. Record his or her answers, too.

Step 4
Compare the differences between the two experiments. Did the blindfolded person make any mistakes or take longer in identifying the flavors?

🌀 We are used to seeing foods in certain colors, and this helps identify their flavors.

The chemical factor

Find out if saliva helps you when it comes to tasting food.

You will need:
• Paper towel
• Selection of dry foods, such as cookies, cakes, or crackers
• Two friends

Step 1
Pat the tongue of one of your volunteers dry with the paper towel so that no part of the tongue's top side has saliva on it. The second person can taste the food as normal.

🌀 Chemicals from food can reach your taste buds only if they have been dissolved in saliva.

Step 2
Ask the two subjects to taste the dry food and then record their responses as to how much flavor they can taste.

A child has around 10,000 taste buds, while an adult may have only 5,000.

43

HOW YOU FEEL AND
TOUCH

Your skin is the largest organ in your body. It has many functions, including acting as a protective barrier against infection, but it also provides you with vital information about your environment. It does this by using millions of sensory receptor cells that detect different types of stimuli—from the most delicate tap to the sharp shock of pain.

Thalamus

Free nerve endings
Sense touch, pressure, pain, and temperature

Sensitive skin

Human skin has at least six types of sensory receptors. Some are branched nerve endings, while others are nerve fibers that end in tiny disks or capsules that detect different types of pressure, vibration, stretching, temperature change, and physical damage. Some nerve endings are wrapped around the roots of hairs and sense their response to touch and air movement.

Merkel's disk
Responds to light touch and pressure

Hair root sensors
Detect hair movement

There are around 18 million skin sensors altogether, constantly sending information to the brain.

Signal network

Sensory signals from the skin are sent through the branching nerves of the peripheral nervous system to the spinal cord and then to the thalamus. The thalamus passes them on to the somatic sensory cortex, which is located in the brain. The thalamus acts as a relay station, as it does for all sensory information except smell.

Fingertip control

Some parts of your skin are much more sensitive than others. If something touches your leg, you can certainly feel it, but the sensation is not very precise. By contrast, your fingertips are highly sensitive, giving you the sense of touch that allows you to feel textures and, in the case of blind people, to read Braille.

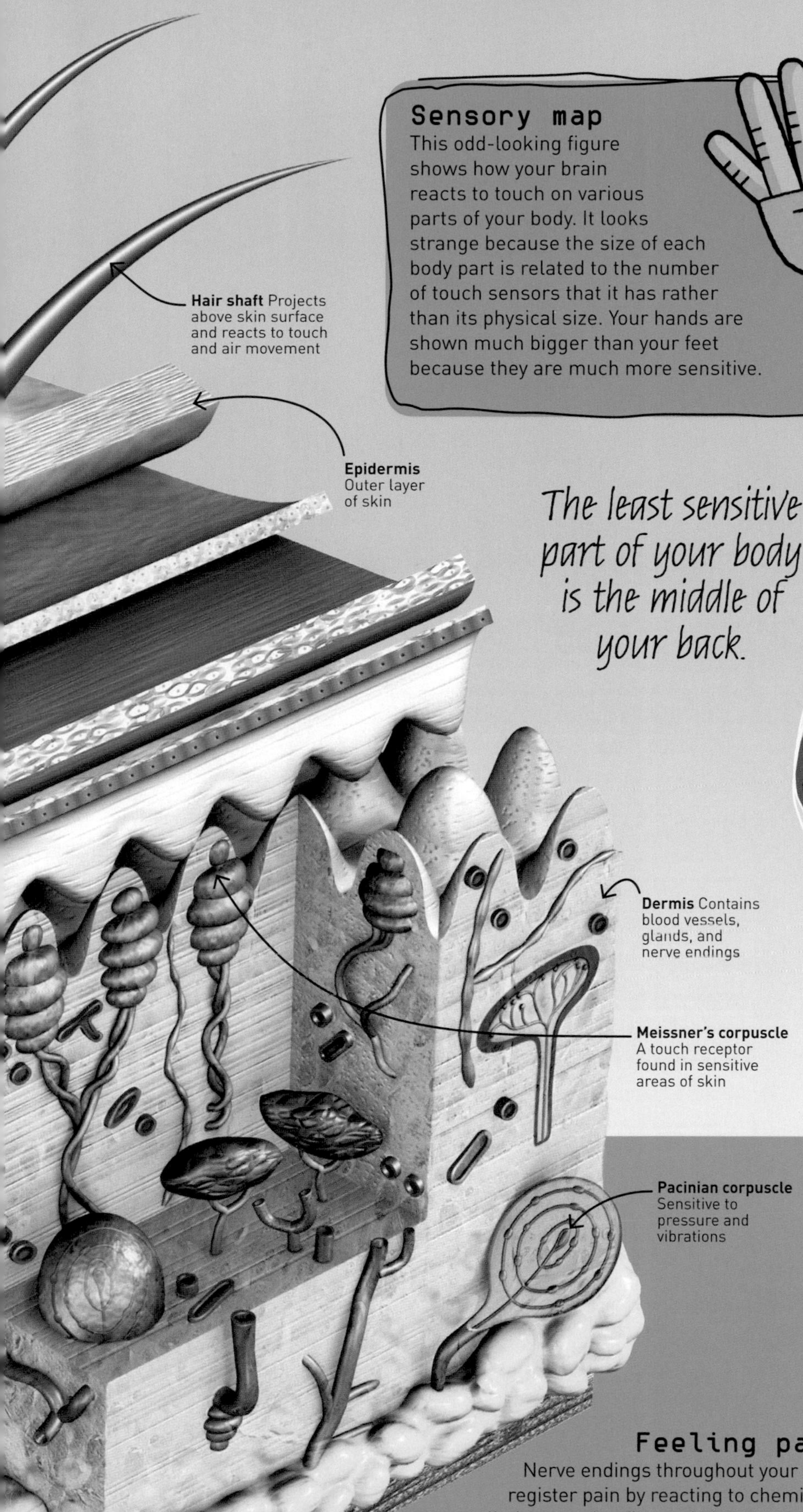

Sensory map

This odd-looking figure shows how your brain reacts to touch on various parts of your body. It looks strange because the size of each body part is related to the number of touch sensors that it has rather than its physical size. Your hands are shown much bigger than your feet because they are much more sensitive.

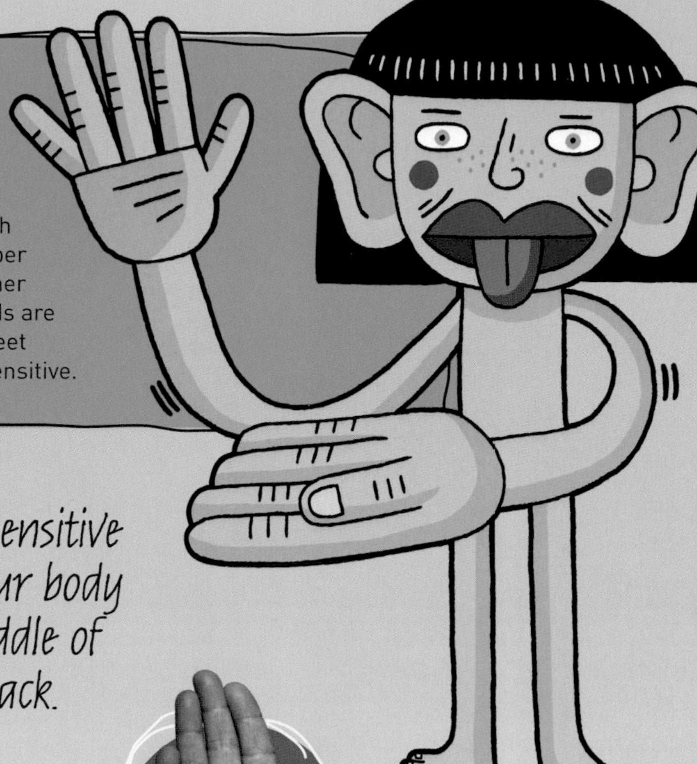

The least sensitive part of your body is the middle of your back.

Hair shaft Projects above skin surface and reacts to touch and air movement

Epidermis Outer layer of skin

Dermis Contains blood vessels, glands, and nerve endings

Meissner's corpuscle A touch receptor found in sensitive areas of skin

Pacinian corpuscle Sensitive to pressure and vibrations

Habituation

Although your brain reacts strongly to new sensory information from your skin, it adapts to some constant or repetitive messages to make them less distracting. This effect happens with all the senses but is most easily tested using touch. If you put a pencil in the palm of your hand, for example, you get an instant sensation, but within seconds this wears off to leave just a low-key awareness. This is because some skin sensors soon stop sending signals, but others don't.

Feeling pain

Nerve endings throughout your skin register pain by reacting to chemicals called prostaglandins and histamines that are released from damaged cells. There are two types of pain responses. One is short and sharp to make you jerk your hand away from a candle flame in a reflex action. The other is slower and starts after the reflex, giving more persistent pain and warning us of possible long-term harm.

45

TOUCH AND TELL

Grab bag

How good is your sense of touch in helping you identify objects?

You will need:
• Box with two holes cut out, or a pillowcase
• Selection of items in all sizes such as a cup, spoon, ball, apple, sponge, rock, pinecone, and feather
• Socks or rubber gloves
• A friend

Step 1

Place a few items in the box or pillowcase. Ask your friend to put his or her hands inside the box and try to identify the objects from touch alone.

Step 2

Now ask your friend to put socks or rubber gloves on his or her hands and touch the items. How does this change the success rate?

By covering your hands, it is harder to tell what you are touching. This is because you are reducing the amount of tactile information being sent to your brain.

Artist at work!

Can you judge the size, texture, and shape of an object by touch alone? Try this activity and find out.

You will need:
• Box with a hole
• Some objects such as a feather, apple, book, and wallet
• Pencil and paper
• A friend

Step 3

Compare the finished drawing with the original item. How accurate was your friend?

We have different types of receptors under our skin. These enable us to find out a lot about an object just by touch alone—whether an object is soft or hard, its shape, and how big it is.

Step 1

Have your friend place a hand inside the box and pick an item.

Step 2

With eyes closed, ask your friend to feel the object and then sketch the shape and dimensions of the item. Ask him or her to describe the texture of the object, too.

We have more touch receptors in our fingers than anywhere else on the body.

46

Your entire body is covered with touch receptors, sensing different types of sensations—pressure, pain, and temperature. You can explore your sense of touch with the following activities.

Sensitive touch
This activity demonstrates how some parts of your body are more sensitive than others.

You will need:
• A paper clip

Step 1
Straighten out the paper clip. Then bend it so that the tips are around 0.5 in (1 cm) apart.

Step 2
Close your eyes or look away. Then run the paper clip from the tip of your index finger, along your palm, and up to your forearm. Could you feel both the points of the paper clip on your forearm?

Your forearm is not as sensitive as your fingers, so it feels as if the points of the paper clip are together—or you might feel only one point.

Some animals have different ways of feeling. Cats, for example, use their whiskers.

Hot or cold?
Follow the steps of this experiment and see how your thermal receptors detect changes in temperature.

You will need:
• Three plastic cups
• Ice-cold water, warm water, and hot water at 104–122 °F (40–50 °C). Ask an adult to check the temperature with a thermometer.
• Stopwatch

The finger that has been placed in cold water perceives the water as warm, while the finger placed in hot water perceives it as cool. This is because the receptors are not detecting the water temperature. Instead, they are comparing it to the previous temperatures.

Step 1
Fill each of the cups with the cold, warm, and hot water. Place a finger from your left hand in the cold water and a finger from your right hand in the hot water. Leave the fingers immersed in the water for around a minute.

Step 2
Remove both fingers and dip them in the cup of warm water. Does your body detect any changes in temperature?

Real or fake?

Anything "magical" is something that seems to break the laws of nature, such as making things disappear or reading someone's mind. Some people really believe in magic, just as they may believe in ghosts. Some religious cults such as voodoo are based on magic. But most of us recognize that magic is some sort of trickery, even if we can't see how it's done—and that is part of the fun.

Illusion

A magician tosses a ball in the air twice while following it with his eyes. But he fakes a third toss, moving his eyes as if watching the ball, and to you, the ball appears to vanish. This illusion works because there is a slight delay in visual data reaching your brain. The brain compensates by inventing some data to fill the gap—sometimes it's incorrect.

Criminal tricks

We associate magic tricks with performance artists, but confidence tricksters and pickpockets use similar techniques. If you can't see how a trick is done when you are watching a magician, you certainly won't recognize it when someone distracts your attention in the street and his or her partner steals your money. So watch out!

Entertainers who perform magic are sometimes called illusionists, because they create the illusion that something magical is happening. They make use of sleight of hand, but they usually rely on distraction and misleading people to get ideas into their heads. This requires a deep understanding of how the mind works.

Magicians practiced psychology for centuries before the word was invented.

Distraction
Most magic tricks involve doing something with one hand while distracting the audience with the other. Distraction works because focusing on one thing makes you ignore other things. This magician's skill is to make everyone concentrate on one card, so no one sees him slip another card into his pocket to make it "disappear."

Control
Another way magicians influence people is by putting ideas into their heads. An example of this is the "pick a card" trick where the magician flips quickly through a deck of cards that has ten copies of the same card. If he asks someone to name a card, he or she almost always chooses the card that has several duplicates.

Magic and psychology
Scientists are becoming more and more interested in how magic works. This is partly because they have realized that magicians have been studying the human brain for much longer than they have. By analyzing their tricks, researchers hope to develop new ways of understanding perception and mental processes—a study that could lead to new knowledge about how the brain works.

MAGIC
TRICKS

We rely on our senses to tell us about our surroundings. However, our senses can be fooled, and we can easily miss a trick if our brains are concentrating on something else. Magicians distract their audiences to take attention away from what is really going on. Try these tricks to find out if you, too, can fool the senses.

The card force

Can you trick someone into picking a specific card but make their decision appear random?

You will need:
- Deck of cards
- Pen and paper
- Envelope
- A friend

Step 1
Secretly place the Queen of Diamonds so that it is the third card from the top in the deck of cards. Write down the name of the card on a piece of paper and put it in an envelope.

Step 3
Ask your friend to point to two cards. If the first two cards are chosen, remove them and go to Step 4. If the first and third cards are chosen, remove the middle one. If the second and third cards are chosen, remove the first one. Then ask your friend to choose another card—whichever one is chosen, make sure you remove the one that isn't the Queen of Diamonds.

Step 4
Ask your friend to turn over the remaining card and then open the envelope to reveal how your amazing prediction came true.

Step 2
Pretend to shuffle the cards. Ask your friend to deal out the top six cards into two rows of three. Watch to see where the Queen of Diamonds lands. Ask your friend to point to a row and confidently take away the row that doesn't have the Queen of Diamonds.

🌀 **If you perform in a confident manner, your friend will be convinced that you are doing what he or she has asked you to do. In fact, you are doing exactly what you need to do in order for the Queen of Diamonds to be picked.**

The magic coin

You need quick actions and plenty of practice to make this trick work.

You will need:
• A coin
• A friend

Step 1
In front of your friend, place the coin in the palm of your left hand, near the thumb.

Step 2
Quickly turn over both hands, flicking the coin from under the left hand to under the right hand.

Step 3
Ask your friend to say which hand the coin is under. Lift your hands to reveal the answer!

🌀 **Because the coin was not seen to move, your friend is tricked into thinking that it is still under your left hand.**

Where's the cup?

Can you make something vanish? You'll need to try this a few times before the trick works perfectly.

You will need:
• A coin
• Table
• Chair
• Paper
• Plastic cup
• A friend

Step 1
Place the coin on the table and the cup over the coin. Tell your friend you will make the coin disappear.

Step 2
Wrap the paper tightly around the cup so that you can see the shape of the cup underneath the paper.

Step 3
Lift up the cup and the paper to show that the coin is still there. While you and your friend are still looking at the coin, move the paper and cup over the edge of the table and drop the cup out of the paper into your lap.

Step 4
Place the paper (which is still in the shape of the cup) back over the coin. Then smash your hand down on the paper to show that the cup has vanished. Say, "Oops, I've made the wrong thing disappear!" Only you know that you made the right object vanish after all.

🌀 **Because you have directed all the attention to the coin, not the cup, your friend's brain isn't focusing on what is really happening.**

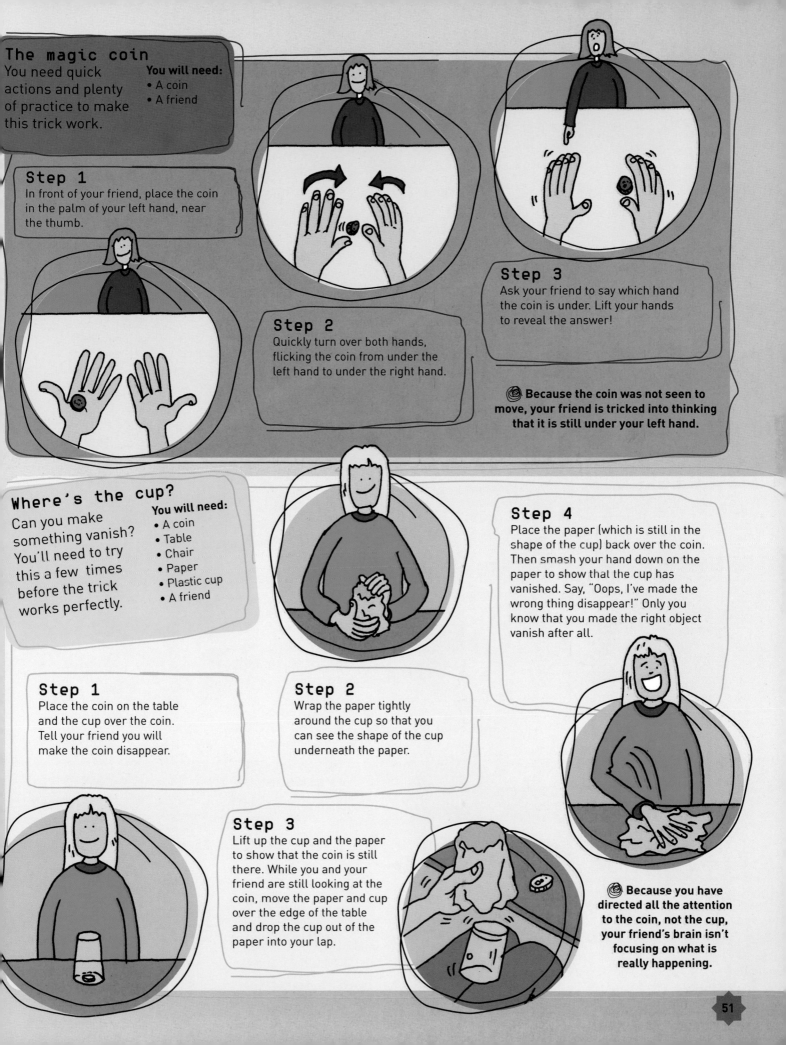

SENSING YOUR BODY

We normally think that we have five senses: sight, hearing, taste, smell, and touch. But we also feel things that do not seem related to a particular sense. They are like an awareness of your body. Most of these sensations affect your unconscious mind, but that doesn't make them unimportant. Without your sense of balance, for example, you could not stand upright.

Balance

Your inner ear contains three bony tubes that form loops called semicircular canals. Each tube ends in a bulge, or ampulla, containing sensors that detect the movement of fluid in the loop—which depends on your body's movement. Similar receptors called maculae detect how upright you are. Your brain uses these signals to correct your balance.

Motion sickness

Intense stimulation of your balance sensors by something like a roller-coaster ride can cause motion sickness. This is made worse if your eyes and ears give your brain conflicting information. Watching the horizon enables the brain to make sense of the movement, and may help.

Vestibular nerve
Delivers balance sensor data to your brain

Semicircular canals
Filled with fluid that moves when your body moves

Ampulla
Contains sensors that detect body movement

Macula
Has sensors that detect whether you are upright

Internal organs

We are not usually aware of our internal organs, but we all get sensations from our stomachs. Some are vague feelings that mark the passage of food, but hunger pangs are more useful. Digestive problems can cause pain, and other organs may also hurt if they are damaged or diseased. A disorder releases chemicals that are detected by nerve endings and relayed to the brain as pain.

Joint sensors

Receptors in your joints detect their movement. This helps your brain monitor the position of your limbs and make corrections for balance. This is essential for actions like catching a ball. Try closing your eyes and touching your nose with your finger—you can do it because you can sense where your hand is.

Elbow joint
Contains touch receptors

Muscle sensors

Your muscles also contain sensors that detect how they stretch and contract and the forces that are acting on them. The signals are sent to the brain, where they are monitored in an area called the somatic sensory cortex. This enables a weightlifter to feel the strain on his muscles as he lifts a record-breaking load—and put it down before something snaps.

Calf muscle
Sensors here detect extension or contraction.

Kicking forward
This action stretches the muscle, sending a signal to the brain.

Goose bumps

When you are frightened or cold, tiny muscles in your skin pull the roots of hairs upright. Long ago, when the human species was hairier, this would have made a person look bigger and possibly scared off an enemy, as well as increasing the insulating effect of the hair. Now, it just creates goose bumps on your skin. But you can feel it happening, and this creates a creepy sensation that can increase your fear.

Phantom limbs

If you are unlucky enough to lose a limb, the brain often retains a mental image of it, so you feel pain and other sensations even though the limb is not there. This "phantom limb" effect seems to be caused by the relevant section of the brain's somatic sensory cortex monitoring another part of the body but confusing its identity. Stimulating this area of the brain then creates the illusion of feeling the missing limb.

BODY ILLUSIONS

Sometimes your brain has a mind of its own. It can stop you from doing something that you want to do or make you feel things that are not actually there. Try the following experiments and witness for yourself the mysterious brain at work.

The Aristotle illusion is one of the oldest known body illusions. Here's how it works: cross your fingers and touch a small round object, like a pea, and it will feel like you are touching two peas!

Pinocchio nose
Ever wondered what it would be like to have a nose as long as Pinocchio's? Try this and find out.

Step 1
Blindfold yourself and then stand behind a friend.

Step 2
With one hand, reach around to tap and rub your friend's nose. Exactly copy your movements with your other hand on your own nose. After a short time, you should start to feel that your friend's nose is yours. That's one long nose!

Your brain uses your sense of touch to figure out where your nose is. When the sensations from touching your friend's nose interfere with the messages from touching your own nose, your brain begins to think your nose has grown to where your friend's nose is!

Hard to resist
This test demonstrates one of the many ways the brain defends the body from possible harm—only in this case, there is no harm at all.

Step 1
Ask a friend to stretch an arm out straight. Then ask him or her to resist you as you press down on his or her wrist with two fingers—your friend will be able to resist the force you are exerting on his or her arm.

Step 2
Now ask your friend to put one foot on a low step (or a pile of books or magazines) and repeat the test.

54

Hopping mad?

One of the best-known illusions is this hopping rabbit experiment. Scientists still do not understand exactly how or why it works.

Step 1

Ask your friend to close his or her eyes and then tap him or her five times on the wrist, three times on the elbow, and twice near the shoulder. Can your friend feel each tap?

◉ Instead of feeling the taps where they actually are, your friend should feel them as a sequence of taps along the arm. Many people liken it to having a rabbit hopping up their arms.

The feeling we call "pins and needles" is actually a common body illusion known as paresthesia. The tingling feeling under your skin occurs when a weight presses down on a nerve or stops blood from flowing to a nerve. The illusion ends when the weight is removed.

This time, your friend will not be able to resist, and you will be able to force his or her arm down to one side.

◉ You haven't suddenly become super strong. When your friend raises a foot on to the step, his or her brain thinks the spine is in a vulnerable position, and it turns off the resistance while it concentrates on protecting the body.

Funny foot

How good do you think you are at doing two things at once? Try this experiment and see what happens.

Step 2

Now try to draw the number six in the air with your right hand and watch what happens to your foot!

◉ Your body finds it difficult to move limbs in opposite directions, especially when they are on the same side of the body. Many people find their foot changes direction, or they write the number six backward.

Step 1

Sit on a chair, stretch out your right leg, and move your ankle in a clockwise direction.

INTUITION

We often believe things without having any idea why. You might get a feeling that you are being followed, or arrive at an inspired solution to a problem. We call this intuition, telepathy, or sometimes a "sixth sense." These intuitive perceptions are probably the result of rapid unconscious mental processes—using either information gathered by your senses or data stored deep in your memory.

Sixth sense

Have you ever felt that something was wrong without understanding how you knew it? This "sixth sense" effect can be quite creepy, but it is probably created by your brain picking up some clue from your other senses and alerting your alarm response without giving you the full picture.

What's up? There's something wrong! The house doesn't feel right at all!

Telepathy

Apparent telepathy is probably caused by a combination of sensory awareness and shared experience. Twins often seem telepathic because they share the same history and thought patterns.

Female and male

Women are usually thought to be more intuitive than men. But psychological tests show that this is not true, and men score just as well. It is simply that women like to appear more intuitive, especially among friends.

Wait a minute! It smells like someone has been baking a cake. Why would they be doing that?

Inspired thinking

An expert chess player may seem to make the right move using intuition rather than logic. But this "inspired thinking" is more likely to be the result of intense study and experience, which enables the player to recognize particular arrangements of the chess pieces on the board. This automatically triggers a memory of the next move, which usually turns out to be the right one.

What? A balloon? I thought I was imagining it, but there's definitely something going on!

Out of the blue

Sometimes someone grappling with a problem finds that the solution seems to come "out of the blue" after working on something else for a while. This is probably because irrelevant details get forgotten, so the main elements of the problem come into sharper focus. The person may also come across new information that makes everything slot into place.

Surprise!

Woof!

Dream work

Occasionally people may even dream the solution to a problem. In the winter of 1861, German chemist August Kekulé was trying to figure out the structure of a benzene molecule. While dozing in front of the fire, he dreamed of a snake biting its tail. According to Kekulé, this gave him the clue that the molecule was a ring of carbon and hydrogen atoms.

Benzene molecule structure

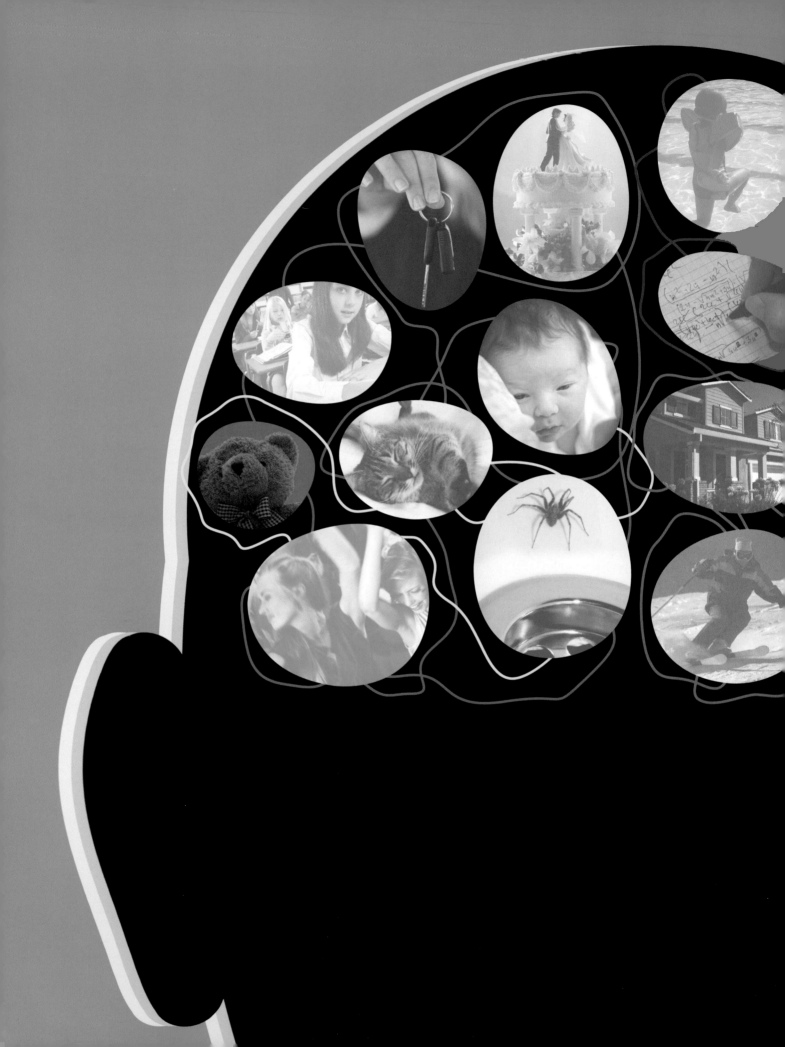

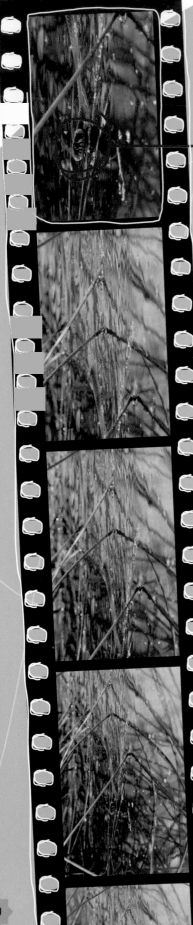

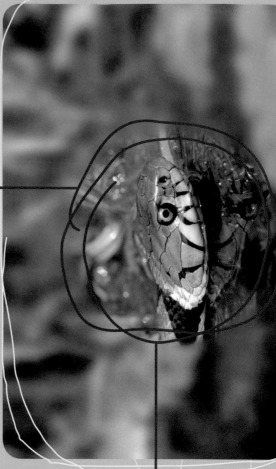

HOW YOU THINK

Our senses are constantly receiving information about the world around us. Most is irrelevant, so our brains filter and sort it, leaving only the data that requires our close attention. The information that we gather in this way is stored in our memories and is the basis of conscious thought.

People who go blind often continue to "see" things because the brain is wired to process visual information.

Attention

The data gathered by your senses passes into your sensory memory. Visual data is held there for less than a second, before being erased if you do not pay attention to it. Attention is the vital first stage in the mental processing of any sensory input. If you don't pay attention, perhaps because you are thinking about something else, the information simply goes out of your head.

Filter and focus

Having paid attention, your brain filters out irrelevant information and focuses on the important data. This is often an unconscious process—for example, a flicker of movement in this pool catches your attention and you instinctively focus on the swimming animal.

Joining the dots

Often you see only part of the picture and have to fill in the rest using data stored in your memory. A few clues are often enough, because your brain is programmed to make sense of sketchy information that might be important to your safety. In this case, the animal's head looks familiar, so you mentally fill in the rest of its body as that of a snake, which might be dangerous. This happens before you get a good view of it.

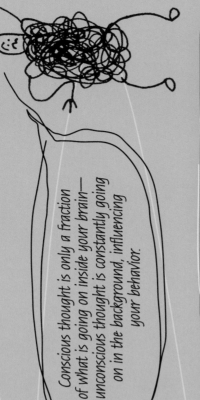

Conscious thought is only a fraction of what is going on inside your brain—unconscious thought is constantly going on in the background, influencing your behavior.

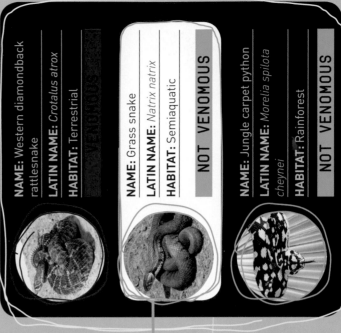

NAME: Western diamondback rattlesnake
LATIN NAME: *Crotalus atrox*
HABITAT: Terrestrial

VENOMOUS

NAME: Grass snake
LATIN NAME: *Natrix natrix*
HABITAT: Semiaquatic

NOT VENOMOUS

NAME: Jungle carpet python
LATIN NAME: *Morelia spilota cheynei*
HABITAT: Rainforest

NOT VENOMOUS

Labeling

When your brain registers sensory data as important, it instantly labels it as a particular type of experience or problem. This helps it devise a rapid response without getting bogged down in detail. So once you realize that this is a snake, you don't go through a mental checklist to assure yourself that you are right. You label it, and take a step back. After all, some snakes are venomous.

Stereotypes

Labeling leads us to create mental models of all kinds of things, from animals to people and social groups. These are called stereotypes. People are scared of snakes because they think all snakes conform to a venomous stereotype. In fact, this is a harmless grass snake, showing that the stereotype is often wrong. The brain's habit of creating stereotypes can be destructive, leading to social problems such as racial prejudice.

WHAT IS MEMORY?

Your brain processes your experiences and all the information gathered by your senses. Most of this data is discarded, but the important perceptions, facts, and skills are stored in your memory. This enables you to think, learn, and be creative.

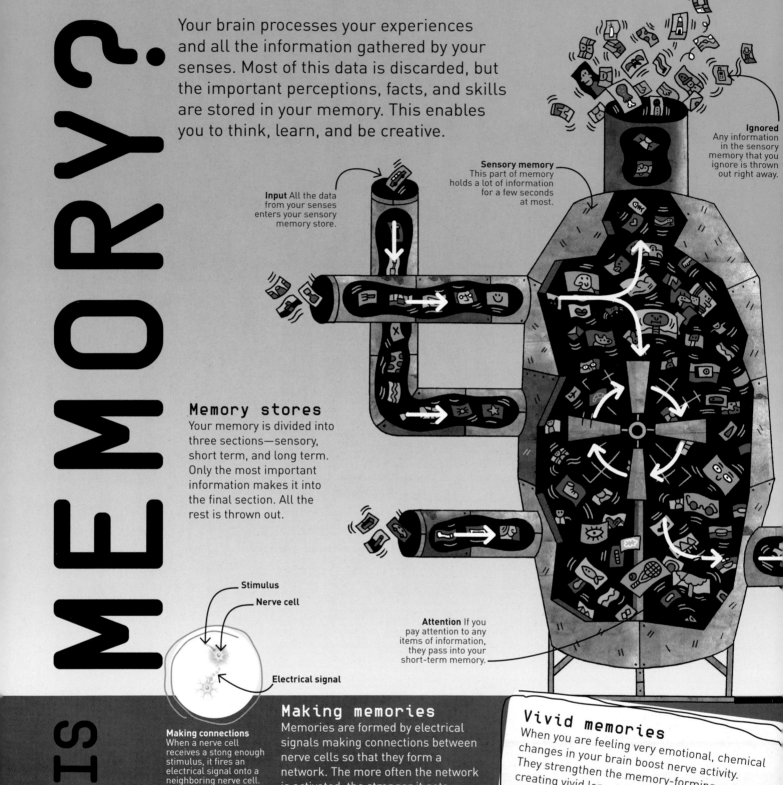

Input All the data from your senses enters your sensory memory store.

Sensory memory This part of memory holds a lot of information for a few seconds at most.

Ignored Any information in the sensory memory that you ignore is thrown out right away.

Memory stores
Your memory is divided into three sections—sensory, short term, and long term. Only the most important information makes it into the final section. All the rest is thrown out.

Stimulus

Nerve cell

Electrical signal

Attention If you pay attention to any items of information, they pass into your short-term memory.

Making connections
When a nerve cell receives a stong enough stimulus, it fires an electrical signal onto a neighboring nerve cell.

Making memories
Memories are formed by electrical signals making connections between nerve cells so that they form a network. The more often the network is activated, the stronger it gets, creating a long-term memory.

Vivid memories
When you are feeling very emotional, chemical changes in your brain boost nerve activity. They strengthen the memory-forming process, creating vivid long-term memories. This is why you often have unusually clear recall of events that you experienced in a state of high emotion.

Permanent bond

Links form
The more the linked cells are stimulated, the stronger the bond becomes.

Memory web
The signals continue to fire until a web of nerve cells is formed. This represents a single memory.

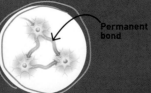

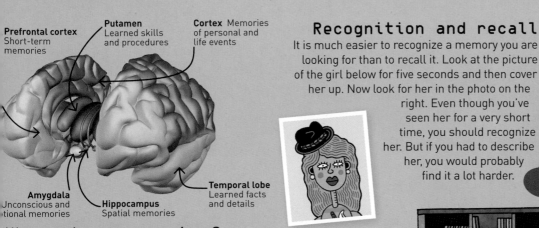

Prefrontal cortex Short-term memories

Putamen Learned skills and procedures

Cortex Memories of personal and life events

Amygdala Unconscious and tional memories

Hippocampus Spatial memories

Temporal lobe Learned facts and details

Where do we remember?
The cortex and hippocampus are the main areas of the brain responsible for memory, but different parts of the brain store different types of memories.

Recognition and recall
It is much easier to recognize a memory you are looking for than to recall it. Look at the picture of the girl below for five seconds and then cover her up. Now look for her in the photo on the right. Even though you've seen her for a very short time, you should recognize her. But if you had to describe her, you would probably find it a lot harder.

Use it or lose it
If you don't think about the data in short-term memory, it is lost after around 20 seconds.

Very few people can remember anything from before the age of three.

Short-term memory
This has limited space, and information is soon lost if you don't think about it enough to pass it on to long-term memory.

Long-term memory
Any information that enters your long-term memory is carefully filed away so that you can easily recall it.

Involuntary recall
Have you ever found yourself smelling something and suddenly remembering a certain time or place very strongly? This sensation is called involuntary recall, because your brain has retrieved the memory by itself, without any prompting from your conscious mind. Sounds and sights can also cause this, but smells are especially powerful, perhaps because the part of your brain that processes scent is closely linked to your memory.

IMPROVE YOUR MEMORY

You can commit information to long-term memory by repeating it. This process is called rehearsal.

It's easy to forget things. It may happen within seconds if short-term memories are not retained by reviewing them several times or by linking them to what you already know. You can also use special techniques to memorize things that would otherwise be very difficult to remember.

Pay attention!
How many times have you been asked to do that? If you want to take in information, it is vital to concentrate and not allow yourself to be distracted. If you don't pay attention, the information will never enter your short-term memory, which is the first stage of memorization. You can't remember something that you never even knew.

Making connections
You can improve your memory by linking new ideas to things you know already. This process slots the information into your long-term memory and makes you think more deeply about its significance. This is a very important form of learning and is called association.

Mnemonics takes its name from Mnemosyne, the Greek goddess of memory.

Chunking
Some of the things you try to memorize mean nothing to you. They may be isolated facts or strings of numbers. Short-term memory has a limit of around five items, so it helps to divide up long sequences of data into smaller, more easily remembered "chunks" of three or four items each. Most people remember telephone numbers in this way.

Mnemonics
One trick for remembering random sequences of words is to use their initial letters to make up a sentence, or mnemonic. For example, "mad vipers eat many jungle snacks using nails" gives the sequence of the planets starting with Mercury, the planet closest to the Sun. It's a ridiculous sentence, but these are sometimes the most memorable.

Mercury	Mad
Venus	Vipers
Earth	Eat
Mars	Many
Jupiter	Jungle
Saturn	Snacks
Uranus	Using
Neptune	Nails

Trip method

One way to memorize a list is to visualize a trip that you often take. Link each landmark on the trip with an item on your list—the stranger the result, the easier it is to remember! Then go through the trip in your head to remember the items.

This is a vacation to-do list, and here is how to picture each of the items with a landmark on a walk to school:

1. Find a book to read
2. Pack your sunglasses
3. Mail a letter
4. Buy some toothpaste
5. Hang your laundry
6. Remember your sun hat
7. Buy dog food
8. Get a haircut

1. Tree
The leaves of the tree are pages from a book. Find a good book to read on vacation.

2. Sunflower
A flower is wearing your sunglasses. Remember to pack them in your bag.

3. Sign
The sign has turned into an envelope reminding you to mail a letter.

4. Bridge
There's a tube of toothpaste floating under the bridge. You need to buy toothpaste.

SCHOOL

6. Scarecrow
The scarecrow has your sun hat on its head. Remember to take your hat on vacation with you.

5. Flags
The flying flags have become socks. You need to hang your laundry.

8. Bush
The bush is getting a haircut, and you need to get one, too!

7. Wall
Imagine your dog running along the wall. Remember to buy dog food.

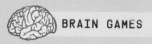

Memory span

Your short-term memory can store a certain amount of information for a limited time. This game reveals your brain's ability to remember numbers and words. You may be surprised at your own abilities.

Step 1

Starting at the top, read out loud each line of numbers, one at a time. Cover up the line and then try to repeat the numbers. Work your way down the list until you can't remember them all.

🌀 **Most people can hold only seven numbers at a time in their short-term memory, so good job if you could remember more.**

438
7209
18546
907513
2146307
50918243
480759162
1728406395

These games test your capacity for storing numbers, words, and visual information in your memory. They also show the two different ways we remember—recall and recognition. Recall is finding information in your memory when you need it. Recognition is knowing something when you see it.

DO YOU REMEMBER?

Visual memory

How good is your memory for visual images? Study these 16 pictures for 45 seconds. Then close the book and write down as many as you can. How well did you do?

🌀 **You've done well if you have remembered more than half the objects. More than 12 is an excellent result.**

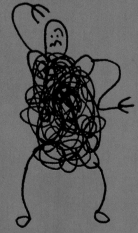

Step 2

Now read out these words, one line at a time. Cover up the line and try to repeat the words. Continue down the list until your memory fails.

🌀 **Most people are better at remembering words than numbers. If you can repeat a string of eight words you have done very well.**

Bed, lamp, rug

Fork, plate, glass, table

Spider, tree, bird, flower, dog

Pencil, scissors, chair, book, fish, clock

Pond, moon, star, grass, worm, bike, stone

Drum, bell, ball, racket, rope, box, net, pole

Eye, leg, arm, foot, head, ear, toe, hair, nose

Bread, milk, cookie, plate, bowl, plum, spoon, apple, banana, orange

Recognition vs. recall

This game clearly shows you the difference between recognizing and recalling information.

Step 1

First test your recognition skills. Below are ten countries and ten capital cities. In 30 seconds, see how many you can match up and then turn to page 186 to check your answers.

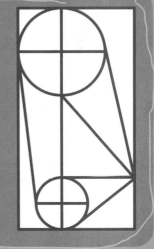

COUNTRIES	CAPITALS
Israel	New Delhi
France	Ottowa
India	Berlin
Russia	Prague
Czech Republic	Copenhagen
Germany	Jerusalem
Afghanistan	Buenos Aires
Canada	Kabul
Denmark	Paris
Argentina	Moscow

Step 2

Here are another ten countries, but this time you need to try to recall their capital cities in 30 seconds. Check your answers again and then compare your two scores.

Spain
Ireland
China
Sweden
Iraq
Netherlands
Japan
Italy
Egypt
Greece

🌀 **Most people get a better score for recognition than recall. This is because having a list of possible answers gives your brain a shortcut to finding the information stored in your memory.**

An artistic eye

Do you have a good memory for remembering visual detail? Try this test and see.

Step 1

Look at the picture right and closely study it for two minutes. You may find it helpful to draw it. Then cover up the picture and try to draw it from memory. When you think you've finished, compare your drawing to the picture and give yourself a point for every line you got right.

Step 2

Now do the same with this picture, left, but this time look for familiar shapes or patterns. For example, does it look like a kite? Again, after two minutes cover up the picture and try to draw it. Figure out your score again and compare it with the previous one.

🌀 **You probably did better in the second test than the first because associating the lines with familiar shapes makes them easier to remember.**

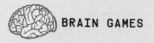

PAYING ATTENTION

Spot the difference
How is your eye for detail? Look at these two pictures and see if you can spot ten differences between them. Turn to page 186 to see if you got them all.

Do you have a good memory for detail? These games will put your short-term memory to work, first testing how well you remember the detail of a story and then how sharp your eye and brain are at spotting visual differences. Remember, none of the information will go into your memory unless you really focus your attention on the exercise.

Important details
How well do you focus on details when you read? To find out, read this story through carefully, but only once, then see if you can answer the questions below.

66 At last the backyard looked perfect. Jenny admired the orange lanterns hanging from the trees as they glowed in the fading light and the pretty tables dotted around the yard, decorated with candles and pink roses. There was a table laden with champagne, a white chocolate cake, a whole salmon, and a tall pyramid of strawberries.

Jenny began to feel excited. Her parents had no idea about the party. They thought they were just going to the movies.

Suddenly, she heard a familiar noise that filled her with alarm—a dog panting. Chester! She had locked him in the kitchen. How had he gotten out? A big, muddy, wet, and very smelly dog raced up and proudly dropped a dead fish at her feet. Jenny knew where that had come from—the Johnsons' pond next door. She groaned and tried to grab Chester's collar, but he leaped away. Between two tables he shook his fur, splattering them both with mud and grass. Then he spotted—or probably smelled—the food table and raced up to it. Paws on the table, he took a bite of the salmon as a hundred strawberries tumbled to the ground. 99

What's missing?

This game reveals how quickly information can disappear from your short-term memory.

Step 1
Study the 14 objects on the tray for 30 seconds, and then cover the picture.

Step 2
Now look at the tray below. Five items have been removed—but which ones? Uncover the picture above and see if you were right. Did you get them all?

Questions

1 What time of day is it?

2 How were the tables decorated?

3 What flavor was the cake?

4 Who was the party for?

5 Where did Jenny think Chester was?

6 What is the last name of Jenny's neighbors?

Look back at the story to check your answers. If you got five right you've done well. A good way to help remember detail is to picture what's happening in the story in your head.

Who's who?
How good are you at spotting tiny differences in patterns? Try solving this problem and see.

Freddy, a much-loved pet tortoise, above right, has gone missing. A reward has been offered for his return, and the four tortoises below have been handed in. But which one is Freddy? Turn to page 186 to find out if you are right.

A

B

C

D

Numbers and pictures

Associating numbers with similar-shaped pictures, can make it easier to remember phone numbers, a number used on a padlock or a number or an important date, or a number can help you for example. Number pictures can also help you remember lists. This is how the technique works.

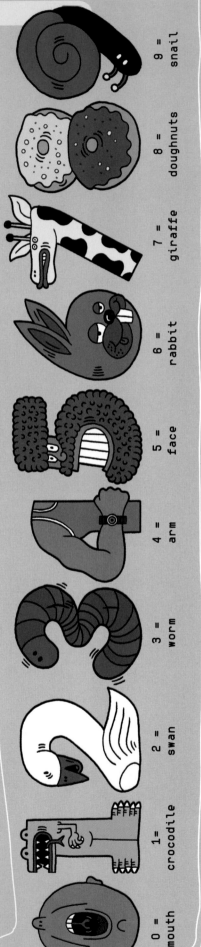

0 =	1=	2 =	3 =	4 =	5 =	6 =	7 =	8 =	9 =
mouth	crocodile	swan	worm	arm	face	rabbit	giraffe	doughnuts	snail

Step 1

Study the number pictures we've created below and try to memorize them. Or invent your own number pictures and learn them.

Step 2

Now study this number for 30 seconds and try to "see" it in pictures. Then cover up the number and try to write it down. Did you find it easy to remember using associations?

8371

Step 3

You can also use number pictures to help you with lists. Imagine you need to buy six eggs, three cartons of milk, two bananas, and eight stamps. Visualize the objects on the list with the number pictures—a rabbit eating an egg, a worm drinking milk, a swan with a banana in its beak, and a stamp with the picture of a doughnut on it, for example. The crazier the picture, the better, because it's more likely to stick in your mind.

Making links between objects—called association—is a useful way to remember things that you might otherwise forget. The following exercises show you how to make associations that match numbers to pictures, organize words into groups, or link a person with an image so that you never forget a name.

MAKING ASSOCIATIONS

Forming a group

If you have a long list of words to remember, try breaking the list down into smaller groups.

Step 1
Study the list of ten items below for 30 seconds. Then cover it up and try to write down as many of the items as you can remember. Check the list and make a note of your score.

Pyramid
Twig
Greenhouse
Insect
Goldfish
Tractor
Nail
Button
Elephant
Carpet

Step 2
Here is a new list. This time, sort the items into smaller groups. One way would be to divide the list into two groups—big or small items. After 30 seconds, cover the list and try to write down all ten items. Was that easier?

Pin
Mountain
Tree
Eyelash
Banana
Ship
Castle
Mouse
Book
Airplane

🐭 If there are no obvious groups, you could imagine items paired together. For example, you could remember a mouse with eyelashes or a ship carrying a banana.

Names to faces

If you find it difficult to remember people's names, try associating a name with a picture. If you meet a girl named Daisy, think of her holding the flower. Or link a person's name with an object they might have (Doug with a dog) or make up a rhyme (Mike on a bike) to help you.

Doug

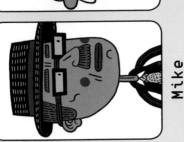

Mike

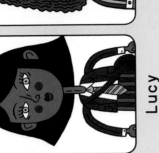

Louis

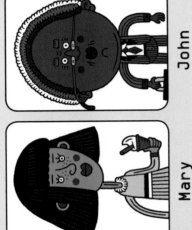

Mary

John

Lucy

Louis

The brain has a built-in ability to recognize faces.

Step 1
Look at the people above and make up your own associations for them, based on the ideas above.

Step 2
Now look at the faces below. Can you remember who's who with the help of your associations?

Einstein's fascination with physics began at the age of five, when he watched the twitching needle of a compass and realized that space was full of unseen forces.

Einstein was born in Germany in 1879, the son of an engineer.

Albert Einstein

When you think of genius, you think of Einstein. This is partly because his ideas are beyond most people's understanding—the bending of light and the distortion of space, for example. He is most famous for his theories of relativity, which explain how the universe works, and for the equation $E=mc^2$, which has become an icon of inspired mathematical thinking. Translating extraordinary ideas into clear mathematics was part of his genius.

This portrait shows Einstein in 1893 when he was 14 and already fascinated by math.

Bright idea

At the age of only 16, Einstein wondered what it would be like to travel at the speed of light: 186,000 miles (300,000 km) per second. He realized that if you traveled away from a clock at this speed, and were able to look back and see it, the clock's hands would never move—because the image of the hands after they moved would never catch up with you. Time would seem to stand still. It takes genius to think like this.

Day job

Einstein studied physics and mathematics, and then got work in the patent office in Bern, Switzerland, deciding whether other people's inventions were worthwhile. Meanwhile he was thinking hard about physics and the nature of the universe in his spare time, as a hobby rather than a job. The fact that he was not working at a university, where he would have had to focus on the ideas of the professors, meant that he was free to come up with his own theories.

Relativity

Einstein was fascinated by the nature of light, space, and time. His conclusions were mind-boggling—that time can slow down, space is curved, gravity is a distortion of space and time, and nothing is fixed except the speed of light. These ideas formed the core of his theories of relativity.

Gravity and light

Einstein's theories said that light rays could be bent by gravity. In 1919, a total eclipse of the Sun enabled astronomers to check this by looking for the deflection of starlight passing close by the Sun. The results showed that the stars appeared to be in the wrong place, so Einstein was right!

Einstein (left) with astronomers at Mount Wilson Observatory, California, in 1931.

Einstein learned how to play the violin as a child, and he continued to play it all his life.

$E=mc^2$

Einstein realized that any mass of a substance could be converted into energy, and he showed that this could be figured out using the equation $E=mc^2$. It states that energy (E) equals the mass (m) multiplied by the enormous figure of 900 trillion, which is the speed of light squared (c^2). This explains why a tiny mass of a substance such as uranium can yield the huge amount of energy generated by a nuclear reactor— or even a nuclear bomb.

Einstein won the Nobel Prize for physics in 1921 for "services to theoretical physics."

Grand old man of science

Einstein moved to the United States in 1932 to escape the Nazis. He continued his research, publishing more than 300 scientific works, and he became a famous figure with his wild hair and eccentric dress. His later achievements did not match his earlier ones, but he had already revolutionized our view of the universe. He died in 1955, aged 76.

Problem

Solving

HOW WE LEARN

Learning is vital to survival. We often think it is all about skills like reading and writing, but it also involves developing life skills such as safely crossing the street, dealing with other people, and managing money. We learn these things through a combination of conscious effort and unconscious reactions, and everything we learn becomes part of our long-term memory.

Find wallet

Take money

How much will it cost?

Learning curve

When we are young, we all have to learn a huge amount about the world in a short time. We learn basic skills like walking, eating, and avoiding harm. We discover that everything we do makes other things happen, and we learn how to predict this—and maybe avoid it. We learn much more in our first few years than we do in all of the rest of our lives.

Conditioning

If an experience always follows a particular event, or does so only once but is very upsetting, this can create such a strong link in the brain that you react automatically to the event if it happens again. So, for example, if you have been stung by a wasp, you get nervous when you see another one—or any insect with yellow and black stripes. This basic form of learning is called conditioning.

Memory circuits

The basic "wiring" of the brain is formed at birth, but whenever you learn something, the wiring changes. A group of nerve cells links together to form a network that lets you repeat the action whenever you want. But if you never use it again, the network may eventually stop working.

Association

You learn by making connections between different experiences and skills, creating a web of associated ideas in your brain. When one part of the web is activated, it fires up the rest. If you decide to buy a magazine, for example, this idea triggers an association with the store, the bicycle you will use to get there, the route, the money you will need, and so on. Association also allows you to link the abstract ideas you learn in your classes at school.

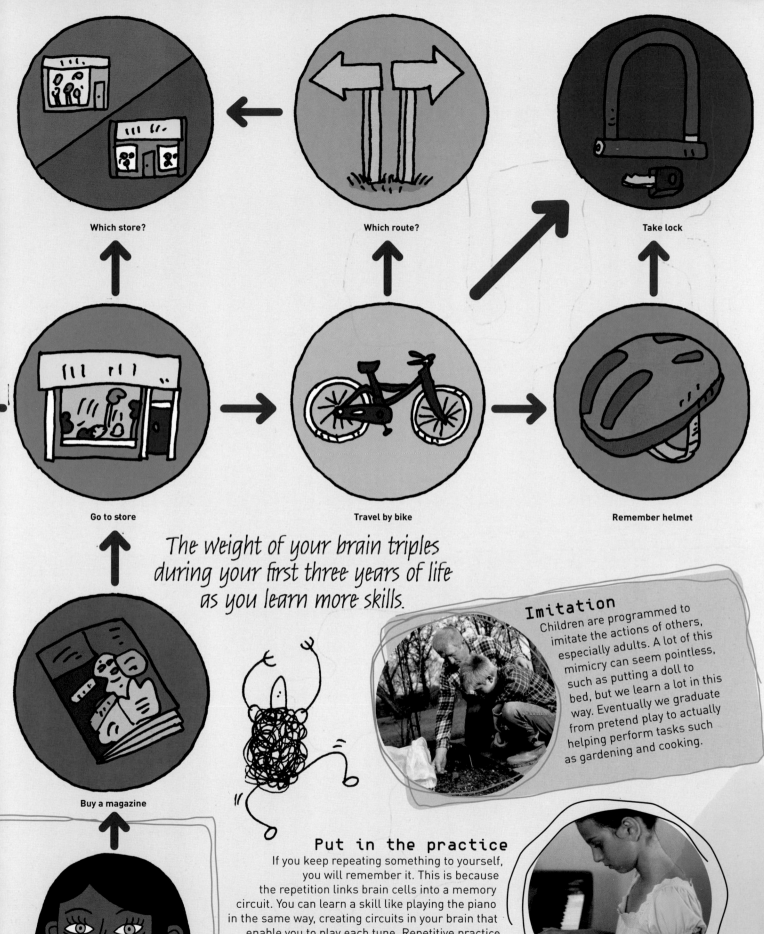

Which store?

Which route?

Take lock

Go to store

Travel by bike

Remember helmet

The weight of your brain triples during your first three years of life as you learn more skills.

Buy a magazine

Imitation

Children are programmed to imitate the actions of others, especially adults. A lot of this mimicry can seem pointless, such as putting a doll to bed, but we learn a lot in this way. Eventually we graduate from pretend play to actually helping perform tasks such as gardening and cooking.

Put in the practice

If you keep repeating something to yourself, you will remember it. This is because the repetition links brain cells into a memory circuit. You can learn a skill like playing the piano in the same way, creating circuits in your brain that enable you to play each tune. Repetitive practice can be dull, but its benefits last a long time. Musicians can stop playing for a year or more, yet quickly pick up the skills if they start playing again.

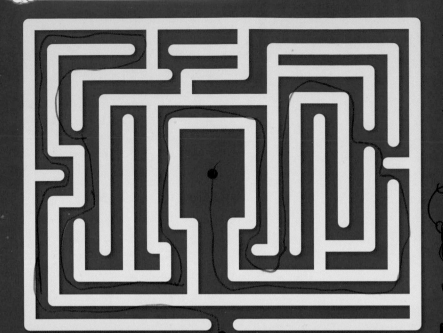

The one-hand rule

To get through a maze where all the walls are connected to the outer boundary, you can use the "one-hand rule." To do this, always keep a hand on one wall as you go—it doesn't matter which hand, but don't swap along the way. Try this method to make your way to the center of this maze—and back out again.

The Ancient Egyptians built mazes 4,000 years ago. One pharaoh even built a huge maze inside his pyramid to baffle tomb robbers.

MASTERING MAZES

The brain's ability to learn helps us solve all sorts of problems, including how to find our way out of a maze. Giant hedge mazes are popular attractions—it seems that people like the feeling of getting lost for a while, as long as they can eventually find their way to freedom, of course! See if you can make your way through this collection of miniature mazes.
If you get lost, find the solutions on page 186.

Right or left?

You can find your way through this more complicated maze using the one-hand rule, too. Once through, try again using your other hand—which route is quicker?

Trial and error

Mazes like this one, where some of the walls are not connected to the others, cannot be solved using the one-hand rule. Instead you'll have to find your way through by learning from your mistakes. Find your way to the center of the maze and then out the other side.

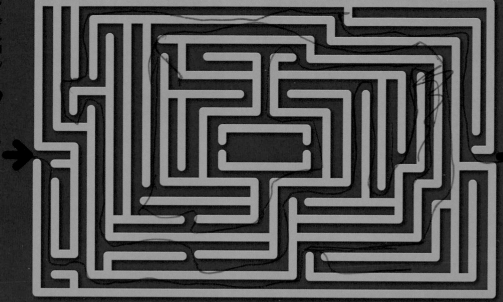

Amazing mazes

The bigger and more complicated a maze is, the more difficult it is to remember all the wrong turns. The challenge of this maze is to figure out the route to the dot.

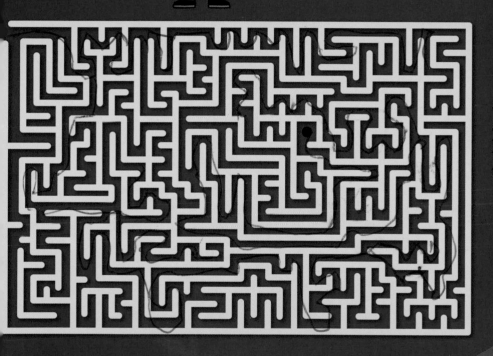

The world's largest maze is the Dole Plantation Pineapple Garden Maze in Hawaii, which covers an area of 137,000 sq ft (12,746 sq m) and has nearly 2.5 miles (4 km) of paths.

Over and under

This 3-D cube maze couldn't exist in real life—people would keep falling off it! The way the paths pass under and over one another can make it difficult to keep track of where you're going—so you'll have to pay attention. Using the one-hand rule will take you back out the way you came in, so to find the exit you'll have to use trial and error.

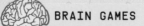
PUZZLING PATTERNS

All alone

Without writing anything down or marking the puzzle in any way, see if you can find the one creature in the picture that doesn't appear twice. To do this you will have to learn and remember which items form parts of a pair.

Thinking ahead

This batch of colorful cupcakes is arranged in a specific pattern. Can you figure out what it is? If the sequence was to continue, what would be the color of the 49th and 100th cupcakes?

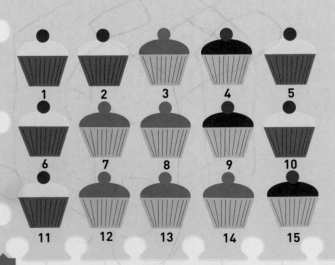

A face in the crowd

The more we learn, the better our brains become at spotting even the smallest differences between things. See if you can find these two musicians among the group of rock stars below.

The world's largest jigsaw puzzle has 24,00 pieces. It takes many months to complete.

Recognizing patterns and making connections between different things are important parts of the learning process. We use past experiences and solutions to previous problems, stored in our brains, to help us make sense of new ones. All of these perplexing puzzles require you to spot new patterns. Turn to page 187 to find the answers.

Missing pieces

Putting a jigsaw puzzle together is a good example of pattern recognition. Your brain has to work out how each small piece fits together to make the big picture. To do this you need to study both the contents of the pieces and their shapes. Four pieces from this puzzle are mixed up with pieces from a different puzzle. Can you find the missing pieces?

Police forces use computer software to help them track patterns of crime and catch criminals.

Perfect pairs

At first glance, these patterns look very similar. Give your brain time to study them, however, and you will begin to tell them apart. In fact, each pattern has an exact double, except for one. See if you can find the unique pattern among the seven pairs.

Spot the sequence

These flowers (left) may look randomly arranged, but in fact they have been laid out in a particular sequence. See if you can figure out the pattern. Which three colored flowers should finish off the sequence?

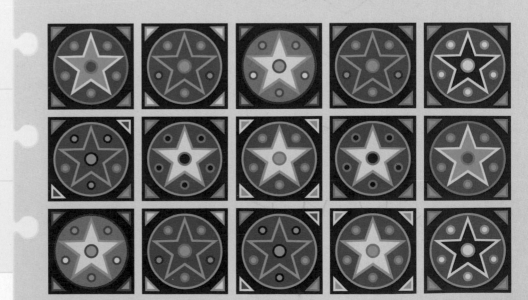

Musical intelligence

This is a form of intelligence that gives a person the ability to appreciate, perform, and compose musical patterns. It involves recognizing and working with musical pitches, tones, and rhythms and is similar to linguistic intelligence.

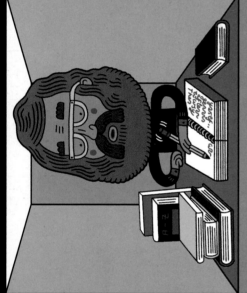

Linguistic intelligence

This type of intelligence involves a sensitivity to written and spoken language. It may enable people to easily learn languages, but it also includes the ability to use language to express yourself and communicate complex information.

Mathematical intelligence

This is when someone has the ability to logically analyze problems, detect patterns, and carry out mathematical calculations. It covers both scientific and mathematical thinking, so it may also apply to people who rarely use mathematics.

Interpersonal intelligence

This covers the sympathetic understanding that is vital if you are to relate to the motivations and desires of other people. It enables you to give good advice to friends who may have problems but also allows you to work effectively with others.

Bodily intelligence

The ability to effectively use your body is not normally associated with intelligence, but it does involve certain mental skills. You need certain mental abilities to coordinate the movements that are essential to sports and other physical activities.

Spatial intelligence

Anyone with the ability to navigate accurately and visualize things in three dimensions is using their spatial intelligence. It also covers the skills involved in sports like tennis and many forms of art, such as architecture and sculpture.

INTELLIGENCE TYPES

Naturalist intelligence
This type of intelligence enables you to recognize, understand, and use various features of your environment. It covers your ability to make sense of the natural world, but it may also affect how you respond to any environment.

What about you?
All of us have different abilities, and multiple intelligences is just one way of describing them. Most people combine many skills in varying degrees, while some perform very well in only a few. Looking at the intelligence types above, how would you describe yourself?

We usually rate people's intelligence by their ability to explain or use complex ideas. Intelligence can also be described as the ability to experience, learn, think, and adapt to the world. According to psychologist Howard Gardner, you can be intelligent in eight ways, combining different degrees of each. However, this idea of "multiple intelligences" is only one of many theories about intelligence.

Howard Gardner
American psychologist Howard Gardner began to question the notion of a single type of intelligence in the 1970s, and he published his theory of multiple intelligences in 1983. Although his theory has been hotly debated, it has helped undermine the crude idea that intelligence can be accurately measured by IQ tests.

Intrapersonal intelligence
One aspect of intelligence is the ability to understand yourself and appreciate your own feelings, fears, and motives. It could be described as knowing how you "tick" and being able to use that information to regulate your life.

Intelligence quotient
Various tests have been devised to measure intelligence. The results are given a numerical value called an intelligence quotient, or IQ. IQ tests usually involve general knowledge, arithmetic, reasoning, memory, puzzle solving, decoding, and analyzing shapes. But they do not rate things like interpersonal skills and may not be fair to people from different cultural backgrounds.

Carver did not know the year or date of his birth, so he never knew which day was his birthday.

George Washington Carver

Carver would have lived in a house like this during his early childhood. He knew exactly what it was like to be poor.

An African American born in the South before the abolition of slavery, George Washington Carver fought racism to become a respected scientist, educator, and inventor. His main interest was agriculture, especially promoting crops that poor farmers could grow for food and other purposes. In the process he improved the lives of people often too poor to help themselves. His achievements helped undermine racial prejudice and blazed a trail for other African Americans to follow.

Determined student

Carver was named after his slave owner, Moses Carver, who raised the orphan as his own child after abolition. Eventually, George got a place in school and later went to college. At first he studied art and music, but in 1891, he transferred to Iowa State Agricultural College, where he was the first black student.

Carver once said, "When you can do the common things of life in an uncommon way, you will command the attention of the world."

In the early 1900s, Carver's laboratory at Tuskegee was one of the few places where black Americans could learn plant science.

College teacher

In 1896, Carver was invited to lead the agriculture department at Tuskegee Institute in Alabama— a college founded for the education of ex-slaves. He stayed at Tuskegee for 47 years, teaching the students farming techniques and ways of becoming self-sufficient. The head of the institute called Carver "one of the most thoroughly scientific men with whom I am acquainted."

Peanuts and potatoes

Carver wanted to improve the lives of poor farmers whose land was exhausted by the relentless planting of cotton— the main cash crop of the region. He advised his students to alternate cotton with other crops such as peanuts and sweet potatoes. He also came up with many uses for these crops, including dyes, paints, plastics, oil, and even explosives. He hoped this would enable his students to make their own products instead of buying them.

These peanuts being harvested in Georgia in 1929 were almost certainly grown according to Carver's instructions.

Carver's fame reached the highest level. Here, President Franklin D. Roosevelt greets Carver in 1936.

Spreading the word

The poorest farmers could read Carver's "practical bulletins"—free brochures with information on crops, cultivation techniques, and recipes. He published 44, the most popular of which was *How to Grow the Peanut and 105 Ways of Preparing it for Human Consumption*. He also wrote bulletins on sweet potatoes, cotton, peas, plums, corn, poultry, dairy farming, pigs, and meat preservation.

Legacy

In January 1943, Carver died at the age of 78 after falling down the stairs at his home. Just six months later, President Franklin D. Roosevelt announced plans for the George Washington Carver National Monument near Diamond, Missouri, where Carver had spent his early childhood. This was the first national monument to an African American, and it incorporates this commemorative bust. Carver was a key figure in the erosion of racial prejudice in the United States, and he blazed a trail for figures such as President Barack Obama.

Fame

Carver shot to fame in 1921 when, despite racial segregation, he was elected to speak on behalf of peanut farmers before a committee of the U.S. House of Representatives. He was mocked at first, but by the time he had finished, the committee was spellbound by his intelligence, eloquence, and courtesy, and they stood to applaud him. It was a great moment for black Americans, and from then on he was a celebrity.

LOGIC

Everyone thinks, but some people think in a less disciplined way than others. They say things that don't add up. Someone might say that she hates all animals but then say that she really likes her neighbor's cat. The two statements contradict each other, so you don't know which one to take seriously. People who talk like this are often said to be lacking in logic—they can't analyze what they say and see the flaws in it. Logic is all about thinking clearly.

o Flawed reasoning

If you say that all fish live in water and that sharks are fish, you can conclude that sharks live in water. But if you say that penguins can swim and, since penguins are birds, all birds can swim, this is clearly wrong. The reasoning is flawed because the concluding statement isn't a logical progression from the first one.

TERIFFIC
TOOTHPASTE

DESTROYS THE BACTERIA THAT CAUSE TOOTH DECAY

Use your head

Logic involves using sound reasoning to draw the right conclusions from known facts. If you cannot fault the reasoning, it is likely that the conclusions are correct. Checking the reasoning is an important part of logical thinking. But perfectly good reasoning is no use if the basic facts are wrong, so you have to check those as well.

Testing the argument

The ability to test the argument is important when you can't test the conclusion. Bacteria are well known to cause tooth decay, so it is logical to argue that a toothpaste that destroys bacteria will help prevent tooth decay. You have to trust the logic, because you have no way of testing the effect on your teeth.

Persuasive logic

Many people use logic to persuade others. If someone says something that you don't believe but then backs it up with a solid logical argument, you might start to believe it. But if there is no logical argument to back it up, you will not be persuaded. This makes logic very important for lawyers and politicians such as Hillary Clinton.

Logic and philosophy

The intellectual discipline of philosophy, first practiced by the ancient Greeks, is mostly about logic, because it uses reasoned argument to investigate concepts such as truth, beauty, and justice. To many people, these exercises are intellectual games, as we believe we know the answers through common sense. But common sense can be misleading if it is based on false ideas. The rigorous, logical argument encouraged by the study of philosophy has real practical value.

Computer logic

Logic is vital to computing. All computers are controlled by long strings of electronic instructions called programs. These are devised by programmers who have to convert their ideas into a code that a computer can read. If the coded instructions are not logical, the program will not work.

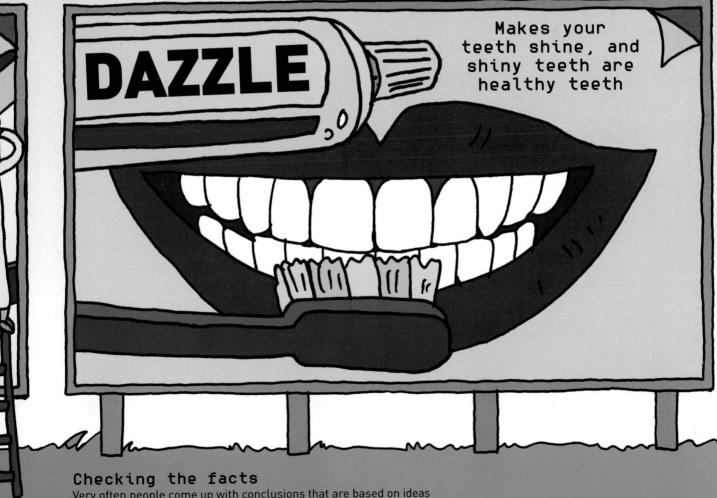

DAZZLE

Makes your teeth shine, and shiny teeth are healthy teeth

Checking the facts

Very often people come up with conclusions that are based on ideas that are wrong. If making teeth shiny really did make them healthy, the argument in this advertisement would be fine. But simply brushing your teeth does not prevent tooth decay, so the facts are wrong. It's important to check the facts as well as the logic.

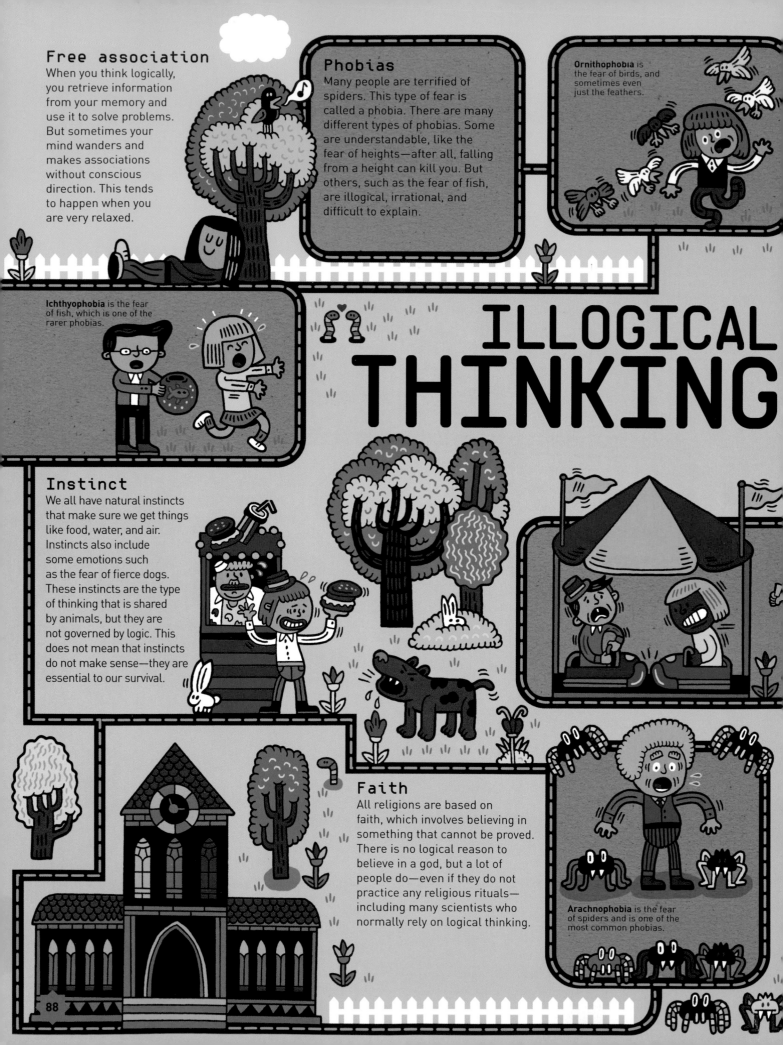

Free association

When you think logically, you retrieve information from your memory and use it to solve problems. But sometimes your mind wanders and makes associations without conscious direction. This tends to happen when you are very relaxed.

Phobias

Many people are terrified of spiders. This type of fear is called a phobia. There are many different types of phobias. Some are understandable, like the fear of heights—after all, falling from a height can kill you. But others, such as the fear of fish, are illogical, irrational, and difficult to explain.

Ornithophobia is the fear of birds, and sometimes even just the feathers.

Ichthyophobia is the fear of fish, which is one of the rarer phobias.

ILLOGICAL THINKING

Instinct

We all have natural instincts that make sure we get things like food, water, and air. Instincts also include some emotions such as the fear of fierce dogs. These instincts are the type of thinking that is shared by animals, but they are not governed by logic. This does not mean that instincts do not make sense—they are essential to our survival.

Faith

All religions are based on faith, which involves believing in something that cannot be proved. There is no logical reason to believe in a god, but a lot of people do—even if they do not practice any religious rituals—including many scientists who normally rely on logical thinking.

Arachnophobia is the fear of spiders and is one of the most common phobias.

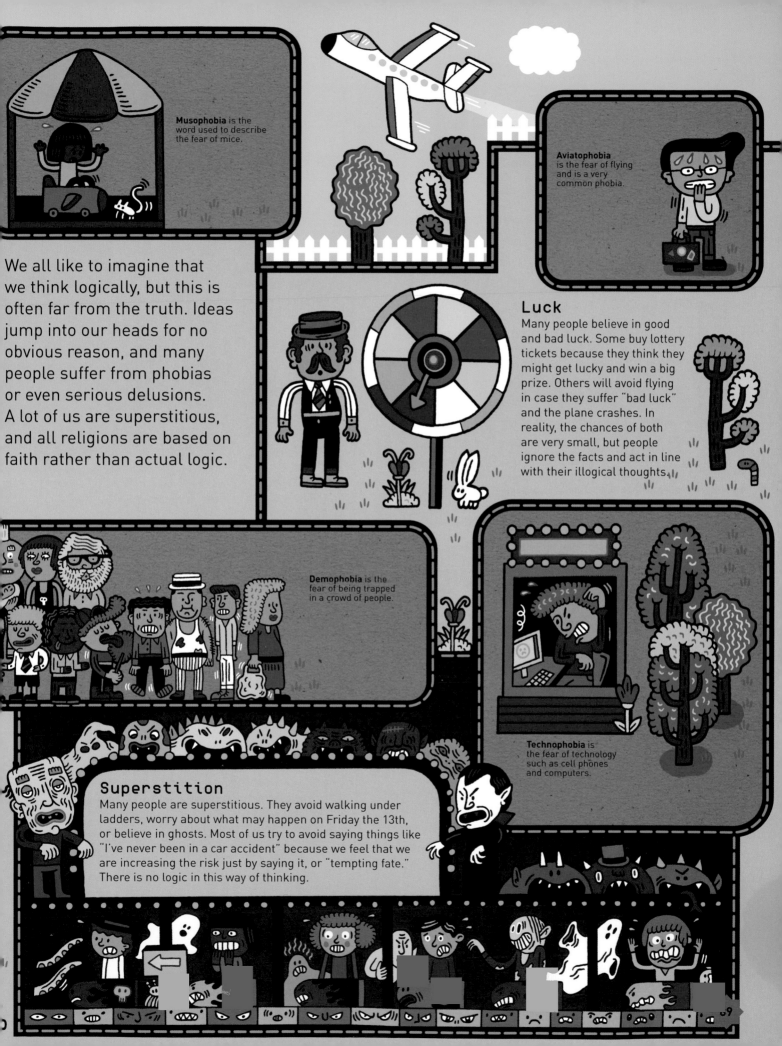

Musophobia is the word used to describe the fear of mice.

Aviatophobia is the fear of flying and is a very common phobia.

We all like to imagine that we think logically, but this is often far from the truth. Ideas jump into our heads for no obvious reason, and many people suffer from phobias or even serious delusions. A lot of us are superstitious, and all religions are based on faith rather than actual logic.

Luck

Many people believe in good and bad luck. Some buy lottery tickets because they think they might get lucky and win a big prize. Others will avoid flying in case they suffer "bad luck" and the plane crashes. In reality, the chances of both are very small, but people ignore the facts and act in line with their illogical thoughts.

Demophobia is the fear of being trapped in a crowd of people.

Technophobia is the fear of technology such as cell phones and computers.

Superstition

Many people are superstitious. They avoid walking under ladders, worry about what may happen on Friday the 13th, or believe in ghosts. Most of us try to avoid saying things like "I've never been in a car accident" because we feel that we are increasing the risk just by saying it, or "tempting fate." There is no logic in this way of thinking.

BRAINTEASERS

Clear, logical thinking is the key to solving these baffling brainteasers. They have been designed to confuse, confound, and mislead, so you'll have to concentrate hard and use sound reasoning to arrive at your answers. Turn to page 187 to see if you are right.

The frustrated farmer

A farmer is trying to use a small boat to row a fox, a chicken, and a bag of corn across a river. However, he can take only one thing at a time in the boat. If he leaves the fox with the chicken, the fox will eat the chicken. If he leaves the chicken with the corn, the chicken will eat the corn. How can the farmer get across the river without anything eating anything else?

It might help if you make paper cutouts of the characters to help you visualize the solution.

Carnival money

Three boys arrive at a carnival on Sunday morning. The man in the ticket booth tells them that the entrance fee is $10 each—so the boys pay $30 and enter the carnival. However, the man in the ticket booth realizes that tickets cost less on Sundays, so the boys should have paid only $25. The man asks his assistant to go find the boys and give them $5 back. The assistant can't figure out how to split $5 between three people, so he keeps $2 for himself and gives the boys $1 each. This means that the boys have now paid $9 each for their tickets—a total of $27—and the assistant has kept $2, making $29 . . . What happened to the other $1?

Find the treat

Janet wants a cookie, but first she needs to find the cookie jar in the cupboard. None of the jars has labels, only numbers. She gets only one guess. If she's wrong, she'll end up with something much less tasty than a cookie. To help her choose, she is given the following clues:

Two at a time

A group of four men—made up of two brothers plus their father and grandfather—is walking to a train station in the dark and come to an old narrow bridge that leads to the station. The bridge can support only two people at a time, and they have only one flashlight between them, so after one pair has crossed, one of the men needs to bring the flashlight back for the next pair. The four men take different times to cross the bridge.

• Brother 1 takes one minute.
• Brother 2 takes two minutes.
• The father takes five minutes.
• The grandfather takes ten minutes.

Each pair can walk across the bridge only as fast as the slowest man, and the next train arrives at the station in 17 minutes. How can all the men cross the bridge to the station on time?

• The lentils are not on the bottom row and not in the middle.
• The beans are not on the top row and are not next to the rice, which is directly under the flour.
• The pepper is not on the right-hand side and has a number that is two more than the flour and four more than the lentils.

Which jar should she choose?

The right door

A prisoner is given a chance to win his freedom: In his cell are two doors—behind one is a hungry lion and behind the other is the exit to the prison. In front of each door stands a guard—one guard always speaks the truth, the other only lies. The prisoner is allowed to ask one of the guards only one question. So what question should he ask to gain his freedom?

Who passed the package?

Rob has just won a game of pass the package. It started with nine children sitting in a circle. A package was given to the first player, who then passed it to the left to player number two and they continued in this way until the package reached the seventh player. This person then unwrapped a layer of paper and was eliminated from the game. The person to their left then became player number one and the game continued until there was only one person left to claim the prize. If Rob won the game, who started it?

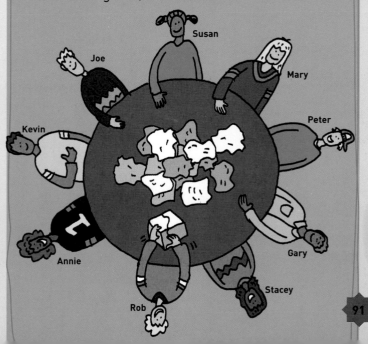

THINKING INSIDE THE BOX

Many number puzzles rely on logical thinking rather than math skills. Sudoku and Kakuro, for example, are puzzles you solve by filling in blank squares with the right numbers according to certain logical rules.

Sudoku

The classic Sudoku puzzle consists of a 9 x 9 grid of squares divided into nine boxes of nine squares. Every vertical column, horizontal row, and box must contain the numbers 1 through 9. Some squares already contain numbers, and your job is to figure out which numbers go in the empty squares. Start with this puzzle and pick up some tips and tricks before moving on to try a few more on your own.

Tips and tricks

	6	8	1		2	4		5
2			3	5			6	
	4	5		6		3		2
		2	9		6			4
4	3	6		1		9	5	7
1			4		5	6		
6		9		8		7	4	
	5	3		4			8	1
8			7	2	3	5		

— Middle row

⊚ A good place to look first is the row or column with the most numbers. Here, the middle row is missing only 2 and 8. If you check the rest of the numbers in the vertical columns that the middle row's blank squares sit in, you should be able to figure out which numbers go where.

⊚ Another trick is to look for sets of three numbers, known as "triplets." Look at the middle column of three boxes, shaded gray. The top two already contain 1. This means that 1 must go in the right-hand column of the bottom box. Check the rows and you'll realize there's only one place the other 1 can go.

Starter Sudoku

1		6			8	3		
	5		9	3			8	6
8		9		7		1		4
7		5			4	6		1
6			2	5	9		7	
4		8	1			2		5
5		1		9			6	3
	8				1	3		4
3		2	8	4		9		7

Never guess which number goes in a square. If there are a number of possibilities, write them small in pencil in the corner of the squares and erase them as you eliminate them.

Slightly harder

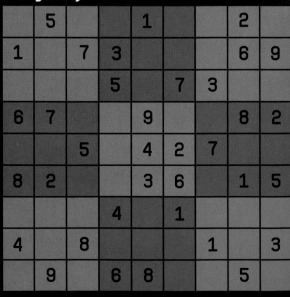

	5			1			2	
1		7	3				6	9
			5		7	3		
6	7			9			8	2
		5		4	2	7		
8	2			3	6		1	5
			4		1			
4		8					1	3
	9			6	8		5	

Kakuro

Kakuro puzzles are a little like crossword puzzles, except they use numbers instead of letters. Like Sudoku, the puzzles are solved by filling in blank squares with numbers from 1 to 9. However, in Kakuro puzzles, these numbers must add up to the total shown either above the column or to the side of the row—remember columns go up and down and rows go left to right. Get your brain buzzing with this small Kakuro, and then try the other trickier ones.

When things get tricky, the two-digit answers are the easiest to try and figure out. It can help to write down the possible number combinations—there may be fewer than you think.

What to do

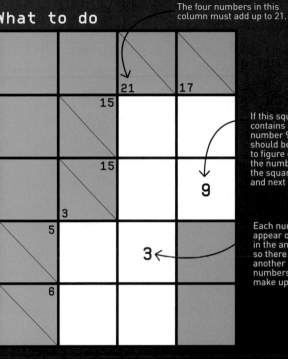

The four numbers in this column must add up to 21.

If this square contains the number 9, you should be able to figure out what the numbers are in the squares above and next to it.

Each number can appear only once in the answer—so there can't be another 3 in the numbers that make up 21.

Now try this

The answers for all the puzzles on these pages can be found on page 187.

Getting tricky

M4TH3M4T1CAL TH1NK1NG

The most logical form of thinking involves numbers. When you do simple calculations, you don't make guesses. You figure out the answers by applying logical rules to the figures. Most people worldwide have devised some way of counting, and most have developed ways of reasoning with numbers.

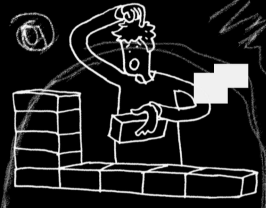

Counting systems

Imagine you are a Stone Age farmer counting sheep. You count to ten using the fingers of both hands. When you get to ten, you put a stone in your lap and start again. If you reach eight, you have one stone and eight fingers: 18. This is why our counting system is based on tens.

Calculations

You want to build a wall from bricks. It will be 200 bricks long and 12 bricks high, but how many bricks will you need? It's easy—you just multiply 12 by two, giving 24, then add two zeroes, giving 2,400 bricks. Most calculations use tricks like this: they are the basis of mathematical thinking.

Geometry

Mathematics can describe shapes such as triangles and pyramids in terms of angles and dimensions. This can be used to measure things like the heights of mountains. If you know your horizontal distance (D) to a mountaintop and you have some way of measuring the angle as you look up at it, you can figure out how high (H) it is.

H

D

The universal science

Today, all science relies on measuring things and reducing them to numerical forms. These numbers can then be used for mathematics that helps us understand and use the science. Scientists devise mathematical equations that explain how the universe works, both on the huge scale of stars and galaxies and on the incredibly small scale of the tiny particles that form atoms. Ultimately they hope to come up with a "theory of everything" that will unite the two ends of the scale—and when they do, it will be a mathematical equation.

Music and nature

One of the pioneers of mathematics, Pythagoras—born around 580 BCE—discovered that the notes of musical chords that sound pleasing correspond to exact divisions of a harp string by halves, thirds, quarters, and fifths. He concluded that math was the basis of all natural beauty. The mathematical pattern of this sunflower shows that he might have been right.

The numeral system that we use for mathematics was brought from India by the Arabs in around 750 CE, and it is still called Arab notation.

Algebra

Certain types of calculations can be used to solve particular problems, and their form never changes. This allows you to replace the numbers with symbols. For example, you can find the area (A) of a rectangle by multiplying its length (L) by its width (W), so the equation is L x W = A. If you know the area and width, but don't know the length, you divide both sides of the equation by W. The Ws on the left cancel out, leaving L = A ÷ W. You can then replace the symbols with real numbers.

$$L \times W = A$$

$$\frac{L \times W}{W} = \frac{A}{W}$$

$$so \quad L = A \div W$$

Puzzling pyramid
Fill in the gaps so that each box in the second row up contains a figure that is the sum of the figures in the two boxes below.

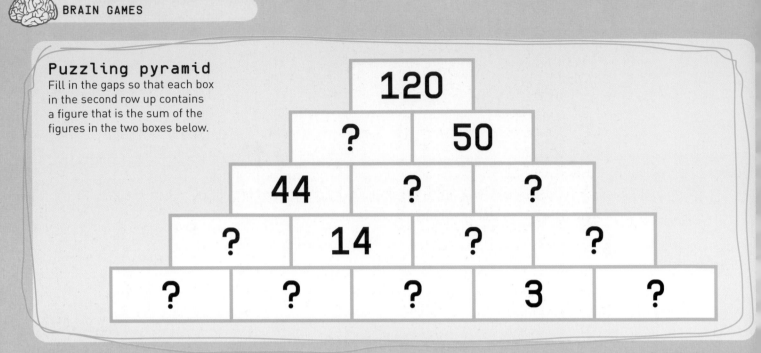

TH1NK OF A NUM8ER

To find the solutions to these puzzles, you'll need to use math—and a fair bit of logical thinking. Some of the puzzles are straightforward and should be easy to solve, while others are more difficult and will require more thought. There are also a couple of trick questions to keep you on your toes. You'll find the answers on page 188.

Only one chance
Replace each of the question marks with the numbers 1, 2, 3, 4, 5, and 6 to make this problem work. You can use each number only once.

$$?? \times ? = ???$$

Flower power
In each flower, the four black numbers can be added and multiplied in the same way to make the white number in the center. See if you can figure out how you do it. What number should appear in the center of the third flower?

Pieces of eight

Write down eight number 8s, like this: 8 8 8 8 8 8 8 8. Now insert four addition signs between the eights in such a way as to make a sum that equals 1,000.

88888888

Pass or fail?

To pass a test, Susan must correctly answer 15 out of 20 questions. For each correct answer, she is awarded ten points, but for each incorrect answer, she is deducted five points. She completes the test, answering all 20 questions and receiving a score of 125. Did she pass?

Dazzling stars

Each colored star represents a different number from 1 to 4. Figure out which star is which number to make this addition problem work.

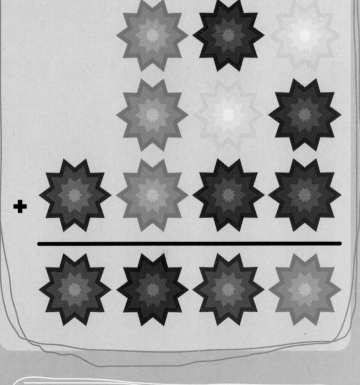

The weighing game

A pineapple weighs more than an orange, which weighs more than an apple, which weighs more than a banana, which weighs more than a strawberry. Study the balanced scales above, then try to work out how many strawberries are needed to balance one pineapple and three bananas? How many strawberries do a pineapple, an orange, an apple, and a banana each weigh?

Multiple fractions

What is ½ of ⅓ of ¼ of ⅕ of 600?

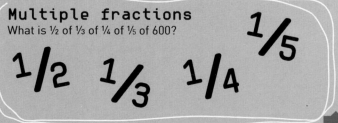

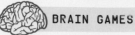
THE MAGIC OF
MATH

A lot of math involves figuring out patterns and relationships between different numbers. Try out these clever mind-bending math tricks on your friends and family and find out how math can be much more fun than you think.

Domino divining

Use basic subtraction skills to discover the total on a domino hidden in your friend's hand.

Step 1
Give your friend a set of dominoes and ask him or her to choose one without letting you know what it is.

Step 2
Ask him or her to pick one of the numbers on the domino and to do the following problems with it—it's okay to use a calculator:
• Multiply by 5
• Add 7
• Multiply by 2
• Add the other number shown on the domino

Step 3
Ask him or her to tell you the answer. If you then subtract 14 from this, you will be left with a two-digit number, which will correspond to the very same numbers on your friend's domino.

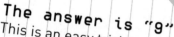

The answer is "9"
This is an easy trick to start off with, because you are letting math do all the work for you. Ask your friend to exactly follow the steps of the trick and the answer will always be the same: 9.

Step 1
Before you start the trick, write the number 9 on a piece of paper, fold it, and hand it to your friend, but tell him or her not to look at it.

Step 2
Hand your friend a calculator and ask him or her to do the following:
• Type in his or her age
• Add the number of their house
• Add the last four digits of their phone number
• Add the number of pets they have
• Add the number of brothers and sisters they have
• Multiply by 18
• Add the digits of the answer together. If the answer is more than one digit, ask him or her to add those digits together, and to keep adding them together until there is only digit left.

Step 3
Show your friend the piece of paper with the answer written on it.

All in a row

This is not just a great trick, it's also a good way of practicing your multiplication skills. Once again, the number 9 is helping with the magic.

Step 1
Hand your friend a calculator, a pen, and a piece of paper. Ask him or her to write down these eight digits: 12345679.

Step 2
Ask him or her to choose one of the digits.

Step 3
Whichever one your friend chooses, you must quickly multiply it by 9 in your head. So, for example, if he or she picks 1, 1 x 9 = 9; if he or she picks 2, 2 x 9 = 18; if he or she picks 3, 3 x 9 = 27, and so on.

Step 4
Now ask your friend to use the calculator to multiply the eight-digit figure by the number you have just worked out. If your friend picked 1 in Step 3, the answer will be 111,111,111; if he or she picked 2, the answer will be 222,222,222; if he or she picked 3, the answer will be 333,333,333, and so on.

22222222222

Math genius Karl Gauss (1777–1855) once added the numbers from 1 to 100 in seconds. He saw that if you add the first and last numbers (1 + 100), you get 101. Adding the second and second-to-last numbers (2 + 99) also gives you 101, and so on. So all you need to do is 101 x 50, which is 5,050.

1 2 3 4 5 6 7 8 9 10 11 12 13 14 15 16 17 18 19 20

Super adder

Perform this trick well and you will convince your friends that you are the world's fastest adder. In fact, the only skill you need to master is how to multiply by 11.

Step 1
Hand your friend a pencil, a piece of paper, and a calculator, and ask him or her to do the following:
• Write down two numbers between 1 and 19, one beneath the other.
• Add the two numbers together and write that third new number beneath the other two.
• Add the second and third numbers together and write a fourth new number below them.
• Make a fifth new number by adding together the third and fourth numbers and write it below them.
• Keep going in the same fashion until there is a column of ten numbers.

Step 2
Ask your friend to show you the list of numbers. Tell him or her that you can add the numbers together quicker using a pen and paper than he or she can using a calculator.

Step 3
When your friend accepts the challenge, don't add the numbers together. Instead, simply multiply the seventh number by 11—this will give you the sum total of all ten numbers much more quickly than your friend can figure it out with a calculator.

For instance, if the ten numbers your friend wrote down were 7, 12, 19, 31, 50, 81, 131, 212, 343, 555, all you have to do is multiply the seventh number, 131, by 11 to get 1,441, the sum total of all the numbers. Don't forget you can use a pen and paper for this trick.

Thinking in pictures

If you have to pack a lot of items into the trunk of a car, you use spatial skills to mentally rearrange them and decide how to make them fit best. You also use spatial skills when imagining how something might look, such as a different furniture arrangement in your bedroom.

SPATIAL AWARENESS

Your ability to think in three dimensions is called spatial awareness. It enables you to visualize shapes and imagine what things might look like from different angles. It also gives you a sense of direction, helps you read maps, and is useful in many sports.

Map reading

A map is like an aerial view of the ground, but with all the features represented by symbols. Map reading is a very good test of spatial awareness. Here, a boy finds his way blocked and needs to find a new route by reading a map and relating it to the real world.

Orientation

Some people have a good sense of direction, enabling them to find their way by instinct, while others may need the help of a compass. The man in the park below is using this type of spatial awareness to pick the quickest path to the ice-cream stand.

Rotating shapes

One test of spatial awareness is the ability to imagine what things look like from different angles. Artists who work in 3-D need this skill, such as this gardener planning to trim a bush into the shape of an elephant. He must visualize the result before he starts clipping.

Spatial games

Several toys test spatial skills. The most famous is Rubik's Cube, invented in 1974 and still the world's best-selling toy. You have to scramble the cube and then rotate the sides until each consists of only one color. To do this, you need to think in three dimensions.

Anyone for tennis?

Many sports involve visualizing the scene in three dimensions. A tennis player must be able to accurately place the ball in the court while figuring out the chances of her opponent reaching it. Some board games, such as chess, involve visualizing how the board might look after a sequence of moves.

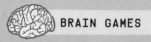

SEEING IN 2-D

We usually think of spatial awareness in terms of 3-D activities—playing sports, for example. But spatial skills can also help us with 2-D problems, such as making sense of patterns on a page. Use these skills to figure out how the 2-D objects in these puzzles interact with one another. Check your answers on page 188.

You use 2-D, and sometimes 3-D, spatial skills when you play computer games.

Up and down

Imagine the man turning the top-right cog clockwise. What will happen to the two baskets of bricks? Will basket A move up or down? Will basket B move up or down? You will have to solve this problem stage by stage, figuring out how the turning of each cog, wheel, and pulley affects how the next one will move.

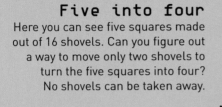

Upside-down triangle

Can you figure out a way to turn the triangle on the left into the triangle on the right by moving only three tires? It might help if you use ten equal-size coins to make your own triangle and move the coins around to find a solution.

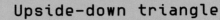

Five into four

Here you can see five squares made out of 16 shovels. Can you figure out a way to move only two shovels to turn the five squares into four? No shovels can be taken away.

Scans have revealed that the area of the brain associated with navigation, the hippocampus, is enlarged in London taxi drivers.

Equal division

The workers, wheelbarrows, and piles of bricks at this construction site look randomly arranged. However, see if you can add four lines to divide the site into five areas, each containing one worker, one wheelbarrow, and one pile of bricks.

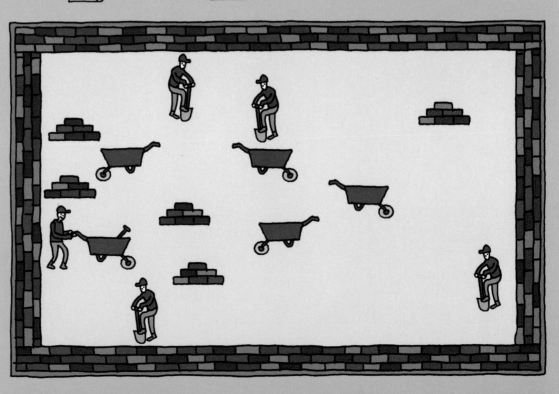

THINKING IN 3-D

Many of the things you do each day depend on spatial awareness skills—walking along the street, or using the phone, for example. You perform these actions so often that they feel natural, so you barely give them a thought. You'll need to pay a bit more attention to solve these 3-D problems. Turn to page 188 to find the answers.

Four triangles

Arrange six equal-size pencils so that they make four equilateral triangles. If you get stuck, remember that this is a 3-D puzzle.

Different angles

Although these nine 3-D shapes all look very different, two them are identical—they're just being shown from contrasting angles. See if you can find the two matching shapes. You will need to visualize each shape at different angles.

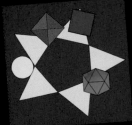

View from the top

The side view above shows four 3-D shapes positioned on a board (clockwise from top left: a cube, a cylinder, a pyramid, and an icosahedron). Can you figure out which of the six overhead views below matches the positions of the 3-D shapes in the side view?

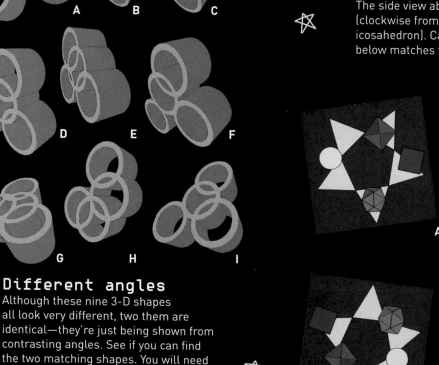

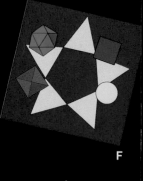

The world record for unscrambling a Rubik's Cube, one of the most famous spatial awareness puzzles, stands at 7.08 seconds.

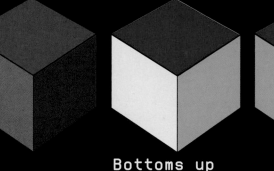

Bottoms up
Here you can see three different views of the same cube. Each side of the cube is a different color. Can you figure out what color the face-down side is in the third picture?

Boxing clever
The fruit pattern below can be folded to create a cube. Can you spot which of the boxes to the right shows the correct pattern of fruit once the cube below has been assembled?

A   B   C

D   E   F

Find the shape
This cube is made up of 27 smaller cubes. It has been split into three colored sections. When the blue and orange areas are removed, only the pink section is left. But which of the 3-D shapes below matches the remaining pink section?

Both these shapes are removed from the cube.

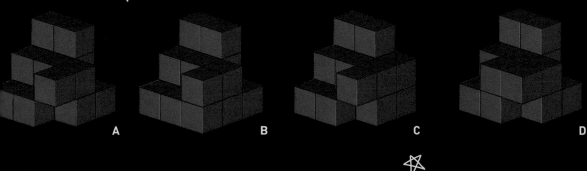

A   B   C   D   E

INVENTION

People regularly come up with new ideas that make life easier and that may even change the world. Turning such inventions into practical technology takes hard work, but the original idea is often the product of inspired genius.

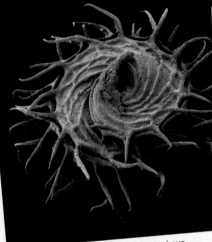

Known as burs, seedpods like this one have hooks that cling to animal fur, carrying the seed away from the parent plant.

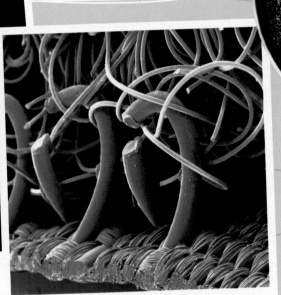

Stiff Velcro hooks (red in this magnified view) mimic the hooks on a plant bur, and catch in the soft loops of a woven pad.

Making connections

Some inventions involve luck, together with the knowledge to appreciate it. In 1928, Alexander Fleming had been trying to find ways of fighting bacterial infections when he noticed that a mold growing on an unwashed bacterial culture plate had killed the bacteria around it—just like the white mold on the culture plate above. He realized he had discovered the first antibiotic drug, penicillin.

Bright ideas

Inventive people are often very observant, with a talent for linking what they see to other ideas. In 1948, Swiss inventor George de Mestral noticed a lot of prickly plant seedpods clinging to his clothes. He discovered that they were equipped with microscopic hooks that clung to the fabric, and he used his discovery to invent the Velcro fastener.

Problem solving

In 1993, British inventor Trevor Baylis was watching a TV show about the spread of AIDS in Africa. He realized that people were dying because they could not pick up vital information broadcast over the radio, simply because they had no electricity. He solved the problem by inventing a wind-up radio, powered by a clockwork motor linked to a small electrical generator.

The Nobel Prize was established by Swedish chemist Alfred Nobel, who made his fortune when he invented dynamite in 1867.

The most important invention was probably the wheel—but no one knows who invented it.

Happy accident

A few inventions are made almost by accident. In 1853, American millionaire Cornelius Vanderbilt was in a restaurant in Saratoga Springs, New York, when he complained that his sliced fried potatoes were too thick. Chef George Crum cooked some extra-thin ones that were crispy all the way through. Vanderbilt wasn't impressed, but these "Saratoga chips" were the first potato chips. A popular snack that comes in many flavors, chips are eaten now throughout the world.

Professional inventors

Some people are so good at inventing things that they turn it into a business. American Thomas Edison was the official inventor of well over 1,000 devices, including, in 1879, the first practical electric light bulb, seen here. His lab was like an invention factory, although many of his "inventions" were developed from the ideas of others.

Fireproof as well as very strong, Kevlar is used to protect firefighters.

Despite their strength, Kevlar fibers are flexible enough to be woven into fabric. They are also used in ropes.

Inspired to improve his son's tricycle by adding a rubber garden hose to the wheels, John Dunlop invented the pneumatic (air-filled) tire in 1887.

Specialized knowledge

Many inventions are quite simple, but others demand specialized knowledge. In the 1960s, American chemist Stephanie Kwolek formulated a type of plastic called poly-paraphenylene terephthalamide, which had flexible fibers that are five times stronger than steel. She had invented Kevlar, the material now used to make bulletproof vests.

A rocket-propelled Fritz Opel hurtles down the AVUS racetrack in Berlin in 1928.

Wernher von Braun

Wernher von Braun was a visionary inventor: a man who saw the future and made it happen. He was the scientist behind the *Saturn V* rocket that carried men to the Moon, and he masterminded the development of the smaller rockets that preceded it. He also had ambitious plans for an orbiting space station and manned flights to Mars. But all this was based on his early experience developing the deadly V-2 missile for Nazi Germany.

Liftoff

Born in 1912, von Braun developed a passion for astronomy when he was a child. Inspired by the rocket-powered vehicles of Fritz von Opel and the work of rocket pioneer Hermann Oberth, he became obsessed by space travel and joined the Spaceflight Society at the University of Berlin to assist Oberth in rocket research.

At the age of 12, Von Braun was arrested for attaching rockets to a cart and setting fire to them in the crowded streets of Berlin.

A captured V-2 rocket is launched by British scientists in October 1945, soon after the war ended.

Relaunch

In 1945, von Braun surrendered to the American forces, who took him to the U.S. Eventually, he was joined by a team of 127 technicians who had worked on the V-2 rocket program. Their task was to develop the V-2 into a nuclear missile. However, in 1958, one of von Braun's rockets was used to launch the first U.S. satellite, *Explorer 1*. This marked the beginning of the space race between Russia and the U.S. that was to lead to the Moon landings.

Wrong target

In the late 1930s, the German Nazi authorities persuaded von Braun to develop the V-2 rocket as a weapon. Yet von Braun always said that he was really only interested in space travel. On hearing the news that the first operational V-2 had hit London, England, he said, "The rocket worked perfectly except for landing on the wrong planet."

An astonishing total of 3,225 V-2s were launched against Allied targets toward the end of World War II—up to ten per day.

Rocket science

While he was working on the first American rockets, von Braun came up with some ambitious plans for space exploration. He devised a huge manned orbiting space station and figured out ways of mounting expeditions to the Moon and even Mars. He later worked as an adviser to Walt Disney, who was making TV shows about space travel.

Lunar landing

Von Braun's big success was the colossal *Saturn V* "superbooster" that carried the Moon missions of the late 1960s. Much bigger than any previous rocket, it had the power to carry a heavy load into Earth orbit and beyond. Von Braun's dream became a reality in 1969 when his rocket launched *Apollo 11* on its pioneer mission to land men on the Moon. Altogether there were six Moon landings—all using the *Saturn V*.

Grounded

Eventually it became clear that von Braun's *Saturn* rocket was going to be replaced by the space shuttle, which is not suitable for missions beyond Earth orbit. Von Braun's hopes for more expeditions to the Moon and planets were shattered, and in 1972, he stopped working for the American space program. Soon after this he became ill, dying in 1977. Yet he had achieved his main ambition of sending astronauts into space—and to the Moon.

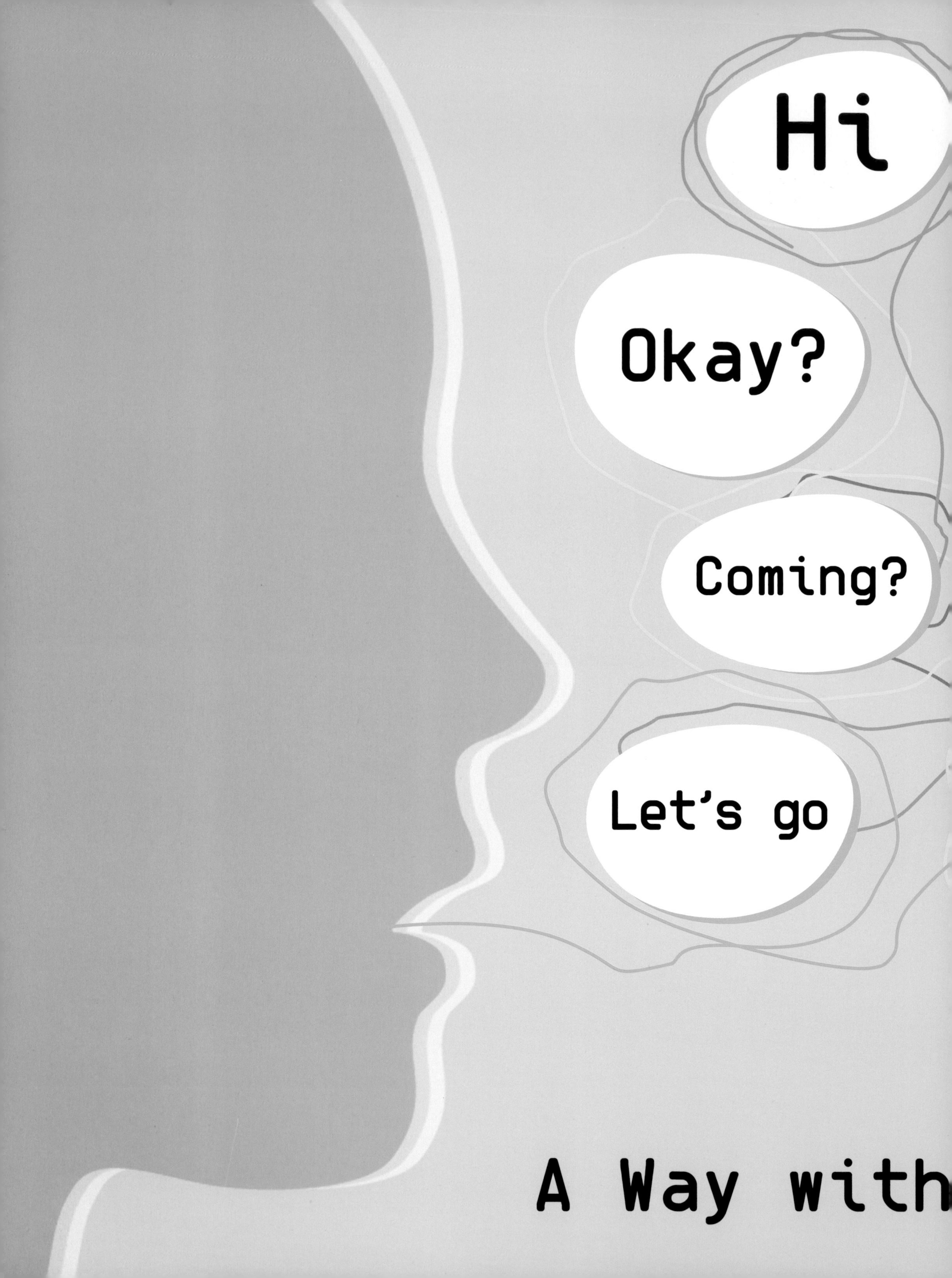

A Way with

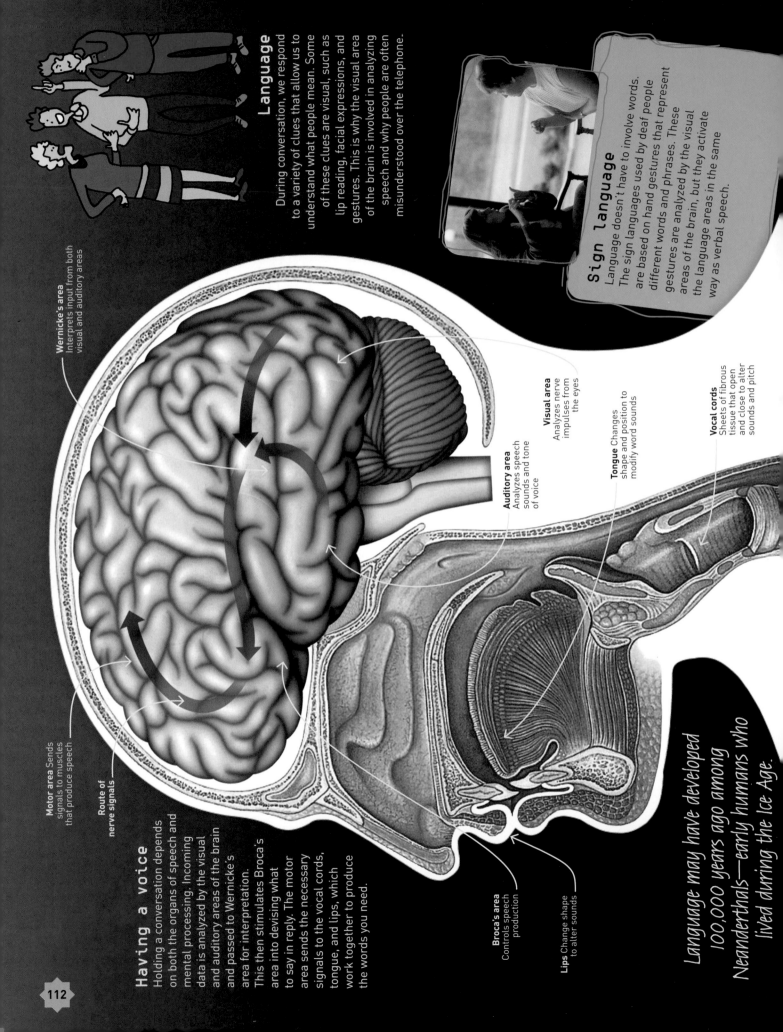

Having a voice

Holding a conversation depends on both the organs of speech and mental processing. Incoming data is analyzed by the visual and auditory areas of the brain and passed to Wernicke's area for interpretation.

This then stimulates Broca's area into devising what to say in reply. The motor area sends the necessary signals to the vocal cords, tongue, and lips, which work together to produce the words you need.

Language

During conversation, we respond to a variety of clues that allow us to understand what people mean. Some of these clues are visual, such as lip reading, facial expressions, and gestures. This is why the visual area of the brain is involved in analyzing speech and why people are often misunderstood over the telephone.

Motor area Sends signals to muscles that produce speech

Route of nerve signals

Wernicke's area Interprets input from both visual and auditory areas

Auditory area Analyzes speech sounds and tone of voice

Visual area Analyzes nerve impulses from the eyes

Tongue Changes shape and position to modify word sounds

Vocal cords Sheets of fibrous tissue that open and close to alter sounds and pitch

Broca's area Controls speech production

Lips Change shape to alter sounds

Sign language

Language doesn't have to involve words. The sign languages used by deaf people are based on hand gestures that represent different words and phrases. These gestures are analyzed by the visual areas of the brain, but they activate the language areas in the same way as verbal speech.

Language may have developed 100,000 years ago among Neanderthals—early humans who lived during the Ice Age.

LEARNING TO SPEAK

Our complex language is one of the features that makes humans different from other animals. A parrot may be able to talk, but it cannot use language to explain what it is thinking. Speaking is not just about making the right sounds—it is about using sounds to communicate. We learn this when we are very young, but we keep adding to our verbal skills throughout our lives.

Noam Chomsky

Born in 1928, Noam Chomsky is one of the key figures in linguistics (the study of language). He is famous for his theory that children have an instinctive ability to understand and learn how to put sentences together—even though different languages work in different ways. He believes that these skills are an inherited part of our nature.

Words and sentences

Babies are very sensitive to words and speech patterns, and by two years old they know around 300 words. They start linking them together until, at the age of four, most children can say simple sentences. By age five or six they can put together more complex sentences.

Second language

Learning another language is easy when we are very young, because at this age our brains respond to every new stimulus. Some children even pick up two languages at once. But it becomes harder with age, and many adults find it is almost impossible (unless they live for a while in a country where the language is spoken). Some people do better than others, possibly because the language-processing areas of their brains are bigger.

Parrot fashion

You can teach a parrot to speak, but you can't teach it to have a real conversation. The parrot just learns to repeat the sounds, and may understand when to say particular phrases, but it cannot put together its own sentences. This skill is uniquely human.

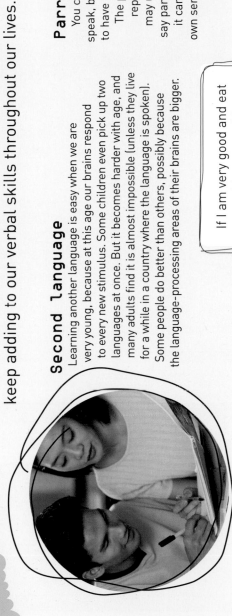

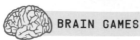

HAVING A WORD

When you talk or write, your brain searches through your vocabulary to pick out the words you need to express yourself. The following games test your understanding of the relationships between words and also show how easily your brain can become confused when you read words in a strange context. Check your answers on page 189.

Odd ones out

In each of the following lists of words, three of the five are related in some way. See if you can guess which two are the odd ones out and why.

1. Sail, cone, mast, cat, deck

2. Stapler, pencil, ruler, pen, crayon

3. Moon, Earth, Mars, Sun, Neptune

4. Dolphin, sparrow, robin, crow, sea horse

5. Tree, run, flower, sky, laugh

Quick comparisons

Figuring out the relationships between words is the first step to correctly using them. Choose the right word to complete the sentences below.

• Bird is to beak as human is to:
eye, mouth, hair, fur, crow

• Eyes are to sight as nose is to:
smell, aroma, taste, touch, hearing

• In is to out as off is to:
up, back, on, below, above

• Pen is to ink as brush is to:
pencil, color, paper, paint, brush stroke

• Tricycle is to three as bicycle is to:
two, four, unicycle, five, one

Blue	Green	Orange	White	Pink
Red	Orange	Blue	Green	Orange
White	Pink	Green	Red	Red

Blue	Green	Orange	White	Pink
Red	Orange	Blue	Green	Orange
White	Pink	Green	Red	Red

Mixed messages

The circumstances in which you see words influence the way you read.

Step 1

Time yourself as you read out the color of the writing, not the word itself. Look at the 15 words in the top panel.

Step 2

Next, time yourself as you try to do the same with the panel below.

◎ **It is very difficult to equal or beat your time from Step 1. For people who are proficient at reading, it is difficult not to automatically read the word. If the color of the word and the word itself are not the same, we say the word much quicker than we can name the color.**

Colored creatures

Time yourself as you say out loud the color and the animal pictured behind the word for the group of animals on the left. For example, the first one is a blue rabbit. Then do the same for the group of animals on the right and compare the two times.

As in the mixed-messages game, it is harder to ignore the word. We have to stop the automatic reading response in order to perform the task, and this slows us down.

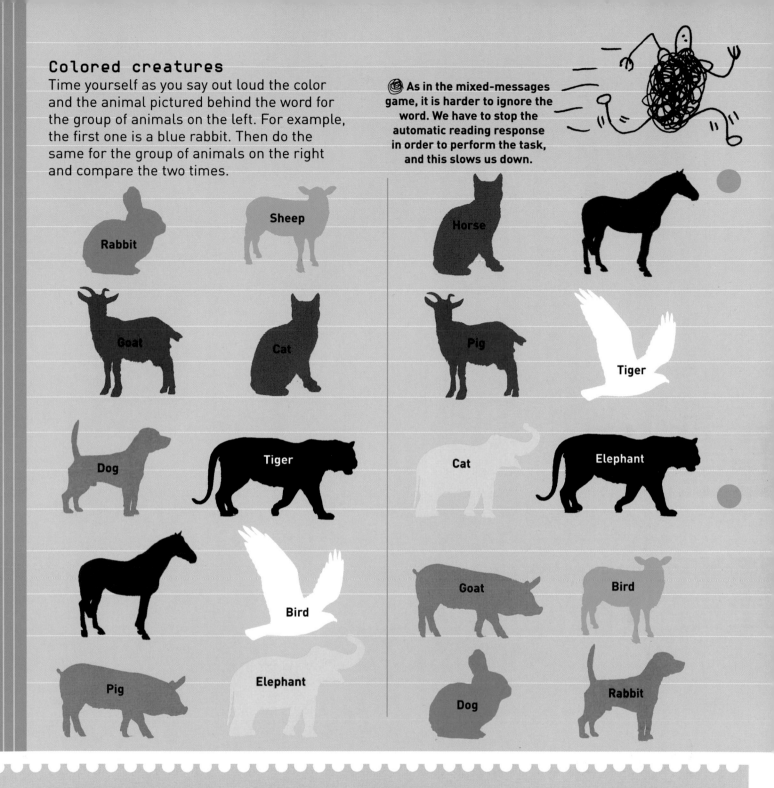

Rabbit

Sheep

Horse

Goat

Cat

Pig

Tiger

Dog

Tiger

Cat

Elephant

Horse

Bird

Goat

Bird

Pig

Elephant

Dog

Rabbit

Like and unlike

This game tests your knowledge of how words relate to one another. In the top game, pick two words from each line—one from the left side and one from the right—that are closest in meaning. Now do the same for the game below, but this time pick the two words that are opposites.

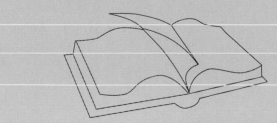

Like

nice, hungry, work
tired, cut, include
scary, trash, party
friend, banana, silly

starving, cat, strong
apple, sleepy, worse
top, fish, spooky
catch, grow, foolish

Unlike

hide, distant, praise
sharp, chew, edge
twist, rational, puzzle
crawl, leave, start

scorn, blink, listen
bite, center, strange
untidy, illogical, test
return, walk, travel

Language and learning
If we didn't have language, we would have to learn everything by imitation. This might work for some skills, but most of the complex things that we learn must be described. The child above doesn't understand the process of buying tickets to see the movie, and will not understand if it is not explained to him. You need language to learn.

Social instincts
We pass information around by talking to one another. Thousands of years ago, a lot of this information would have helped people find food or avoid danger. In modern cities, we spend a lot more time talking about things that don't affect our survival—like these people discussing their vacations—but we still exchange information all the time.

Conversation
Some talking is easy, but a serious conversation involves listening carefully and figuring out exactly what you want to say in reply. This is more difficult if you do not know each other very well, because the expressions and body language that help us communicate are harder to understand when talking to strangers.

We use language to communicate everything, from simple facts about the world around us to abstract ideas about the meaning of life or the nature of the universe. We can talk about past events and plan for the future. Most importantly, we can learn from the experiences of others, build on what we learn, and pass on the knowledge. The spread of culture would be impossible without language.

The oldest known story, told by Australian aborigines, concerns a volcanic eruption that—according to geologists—happened 12,000 years ago.

There might be people living on Venus—we just don't know.

Sorry, but you are talking complete nonsense. Let me explain . . .

My dad was a movie cameraman back in the 1920s, and he would tell me lots of stories about his adventures.

Verbal reasoning

Talking to people is sometimes about trying to persuade them by verbal reasoning. You do this mostly by listening attentively and thinking hard before replying. What has the other person just said? Isn't there something wrong with it? If you can pinpoint the flaw, you will probably win the argument.

Telling stories

In the past, before most people could read, ideas and stories were passed on verbally, from generation to generation. Some people were skilled storytellers, able to memorize long, complicated tales. But this oral tradition is dying out, and most of the tales of the distant past that have come down to us have survived only because they have been written down.

Language and thought

Can you think without language? Yes, if you are doing something like planting a tree or peeling a banana. Our ancestors probably didn't have to think in words in order to hunt or gather food. But language is essential to abstract thought, such as the complex ideas of science, because these things are beyond our own experiences.

WORDS ALOUD

Talk about it

This game is a fun way to check how good your vocabulary is as well as testing the ability of your brain to think quickly and create connections between objects.

Coming up with 10–15 connected words in the time limit shows a good level of word skill.

You will need:
• Two players
• Stopwatch
• Pen and paper

Step 1
Start the stopwatch as you ask your friend to name as many animals as he or she can in 30 seconds.

Step 2
For every animal named, mark a checkmark on a piece of paper. If there are any words you don't know, check with an adult.

Step 3
This time get your friend to ask you how many fruit you can name in 30 seconds. Next time, use your own ideas for subjects.

Fill in the blanks

This game tests how good you are at understanding words in context. Where do these words fit into the story below? Two of the words don't belong, so choose wisely! Check the answers on page 189.

• shock
• gripped
• glimpse
• friendly

• hideous
• bloodcurdling
• surprise
• chance

• flew
• tall
• second
• cow

X-ray almost froze when he saw the shape. Looking up at the _____ birdlike animal, perched at the top of a _____ building, X-ray knew this could be a fight to the death. When the beast spied X-ray below, it let out a _____ shriek and, without waiting another _____, swooped down with terrifying speed. It _____ X-ray in its talons and carried him away before he had a _____ to think. After the initial _____, X-ray turned in the animal's grip so that he got a brief _____ of its face, and he sent a laser beam straight into the beast's beady eyes. The creature shrieked in _____ and let go of the hero, who _____ to safety, ready for his next challenge.

Your brain has an amazing capacity to remember words, often by linking them with visual images. These games help you practice your word skills to improve your vocabulary and confidence so that you won't ever be lost for words.

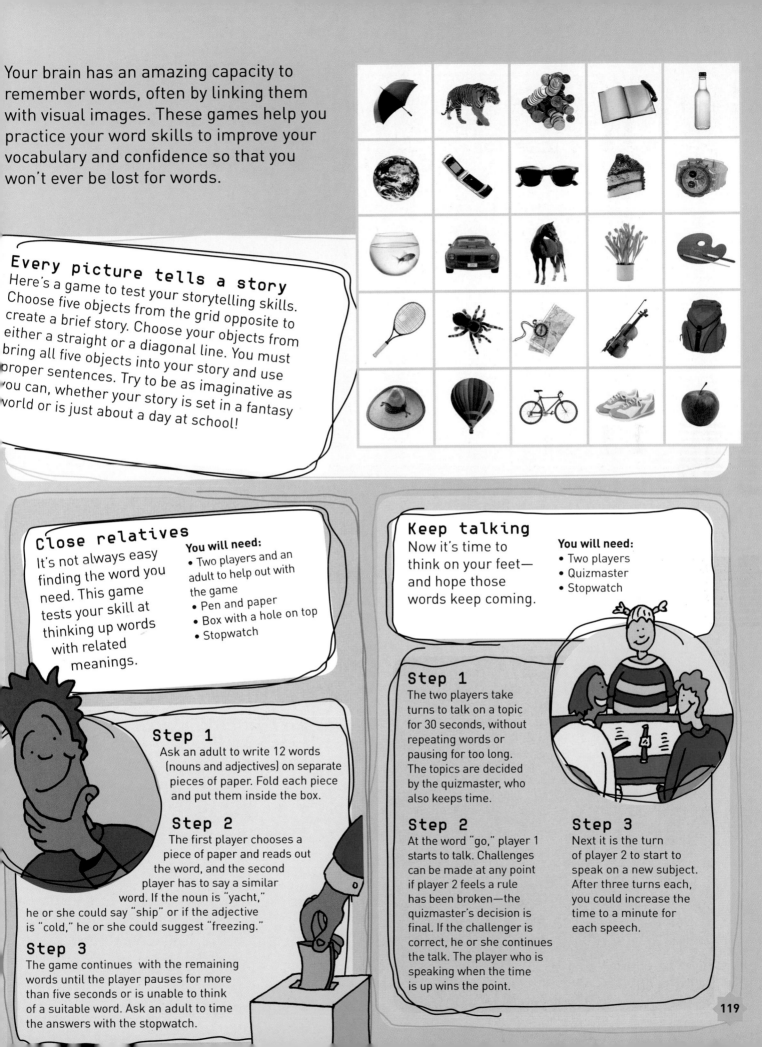

Every picture tells a story

Here's a game to test your storytelling skills. Choose five objects from the grid opposite to create a brief story. Choose your objects from either a straight or a diagonal line. You must bring all five objects into your story and use proper sentences. Try to be as imaginative as you can, whether your story is set in a fantasy world or is just about a day at school!

Close relatives

It's not always easy finding the word you need. This game tests your skill at thinking up words with related meanings.

You will need:
• Two players and an adult to help out with the game
• Pen and paper
• Box with a hole on top
• Stopwatch

Step 1
Ask an adult to write 12 words (nouns and adjectives) on separate pieces of paper. Fold each piece and put them inside the box.

Step 2
The first player chooses a piece of paper and reads out the word, and the second player has to say a similar word. If the noun is "yacht," he or she could say "ship" or if the adjective is "cold," he or she could suggest "freezing."

Step 3
The game continues with the remaining words until the player pauses for more than five seconds or is unable to think of a suitable word. Ask an adult to time the answers with the stopwatch.

Keep talking

Now it's time to think on your feet—and hope those words keep coming.

You will need:
• Two players
• Quizmaster
• Stopwatch

Step 1
The two players take turns to talk on a topic for 30 seconds, without repeating words or pausing for too long. The topics are decided by the quizmaster, who also keeps time.

Step 2
At the word "go," player 1 starts to talk. Challenges can be made at any point if player 2 feels a rule has been broken—the quizmaster's decision is final. If the challenger is correct, he or she continues the talk. The player who is speaking when the time is up wins the point.

Step 3
Next it is the turn of player 2 to start to speak on a new subject. After three turns each, you could increase the time to a minute for each speech.

READING
AND WRITING

Just as spoken language is vital to human society, writing is essential to civilization. It enables ideas to be passed on and preserved for future generations. We can read the words of people who are long dead and learn from history. We do not have to keep rediscovering things, so we can build on past discoveries to extend our knowledge.

Some ancient languages, such as classical Latin, survive only in the form of writing, because no one speaks them anymore.

Adult literacy

Many people miss out on the education that teaches them how to read and write. Unfortunately, these skills are more difficult to acquire as you grow older, so learning to read as an adult can take a long time. However, adults who have been reading for many years can read faster than children because they recognize words without having to spell them out.

Alphabets and symbols

Some languages use limited alphabets to build up a huge variety of words. English uses only 26 letters to form around 500,000 words. But in Chinese, each word is represented by its own character. This means that you need to know at least 3,000 Chinese characters just to read a newspaper. The Cyrillic alphabet, shown above, is used by many Eastern European languages.

Learning to read

Children usually start to read at the age of four or five. Reading involves decoding the symbols on a page, so the easiest languages (such as Italian) to learn are those where certain letters or characters always represent the same sounds. Other languages (such as English) are more difficult, because the same combination of letters represents a number of different sounds.

Words as art

Some forms of writing are so beautiful that they are treated as an art form. In the past, many people in the West learned graceful forms of handwriting—an art known as calligraphy that is still enjoyed by some today. In Chinese, every new word requires a different character, and this gives calligraphy a practical function because the writer can invent an entirely new character to express a particular idea. Such characters are works of art in their own right.

Pictures and words

Comic books have always been popular with children, and many adults read graphic novels that are based on the same idea. These do have words, but most of the meaning is in the pictures. Pictorial representations of words are also used in other ways such as road signs. Known as pictograms, these have the advantage of being universally understood—regardless of the language you speak and whether you can read it.

As lnog as you wrtie the frsit and lsat lttres of a wrod, you can sitll raed it.

Speaking and writing

Although most of us learn how to write, few people do it well. We can tell a story, but somehow we lose the plot when it comes to writing it down. We often use unclear language when we write, which is why so many official forms and documents are difficult to understand. Learning to express yourself in simple terms when you are writing is an important skill.

Jean François Champollion

Some people have a flair for learning languages. They catch on to what is being said, learn how to reply, and are soon able to fluently read and write the language. Jean François Champollion was a genius at this. But he didn't just learn the languages of his own age. He found a way of using his skill to decipher a language that had been long forgotten, enabling scholars to rediscover the lost world of ancient Egypt.

Amharic is the language of the Amhara people of Ethiopia, Africa.

Used to compose sacred texts, Avestan is an old language from eastern Iran.

Sanskrit is the ancient language of Hindu India, dating back to 1500 B.C.E.

Master of languages
Born in France in 1790, Jean François came from a poor family and was eight years old before he went to school. He quickly discovered that he had an amazing talent for languages, mastering a dozen by the age of 16. He also became intrigued by obscure languages such as Amharic, Avestan, Sanskrit, and Chaldean. Eventually he became an assistant professor of history, specializing in ancient languages that could provide a way of understanding the past.

Land of the pharaohs
While Champollion was a child, the wonders of ancient Egypt were just being discovered. The civilization that built them was a mystery, however, because no one could read the writing found on the monuments—the symbols known as hieroglyphs. Champollion was fascinated by the ancient Egyptians.

Keystone
In 1799, a French army captain discovered a stone slab near the Egyptian port of Rashid, or Rosetta. The "Rosetta stone" was covered with writing in three languages: Egyptian hieroglyphs, another form of Egyptian writing called demotic, and classical Greek. But all three were versions of the same thing—a document issued by Pharaoh Ptolemy V in 196 B.C.E. Enough of the writing remained to allow the hieroglyphs to be related to the Greek and decoded— but it would prove difficult.

Codebreaker

In 1801, the Rosetta stone was taken to England. British scholar Thomas Young managed to translate the Egyptian demotic text but not the hieroglyphic script. Champollion took over and used his language skills to figure out what some of the hieroglyphs stood for, especially those that represented names. Between 1822 and 1824, he decoded all the hieroglyphs on the stone, enabling him to understand the ancient Egyptian language. It was a work of genius.

Champollion was appointed to teach history and politics at Grenoble Lyceum at the age of only 18.

Confirming the code

In 1828, Champollion followed up his success by traveling to Egypt with Italian scholar Ippolito Rosellini. Their idea was to confirm Champollion's work by studying as many hieroglyphic inscriptions as possible on stone monuments and wall paintings like this one. They proved that his translations were correct, and they were able to decipher many inscriptions. But the trip exhausted Champollion, and within three years he suffered a stroke and died. He was only 41.

Window into the past

Before Champollion, the world of ancient Egypt was a mystery. Everything had to be deduced from archaeological discoveries at a time when archaeology was little more than a treasure hunt. Once the hieroglyphic system was decoded, historians were able to read the words of the ancient Egyptians and understand their lives more fully.

The Creative Mind

WHAT IS CREATIVITY?

Creativity is about coming up with an idea that is not the result of an obvious logical process. We often think of it as artistic, because painters and musicians are described as creative people. But creativity is an important part of all thinking. The inventions that change our lives would not exist if it weren't for the creativity of their inventors, and "creative solutions" are an important part of science, politics, economics, and even mathematics. We often think it is all about inspiration, but creativity always has a sound foundation of knowledge, backed up by hard work.

Buzzing idea

All creativity involves working on what you already know. When Greek mathematician Archimedes needed to find the volume of the king's golden crown in around 250 B.C.E., he solved the problem with creative inspiration. But he was slotting together many ideas that were already buzzing in his brain.

Lucky break

Some breakthroughs are the result of lucky accidents, but creative people make their own luck. When Archimedes took a bath, he noticed that the water level rose when he got into it. He was already puzzling over ways of measuring volume and saw that the change was caused by the submerged volume of his body.

Scientist Charles Darwin came up with many of his best ideas while walking around his big garden.

According to inventor Thomas Edison, "Genius is one percent inspiration and 99 percent perspiration."

127

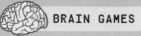

A dotty challenge

Can you draw four straight lines, without lifting your pen from the page, to connect all the red dots? You will need to think outside the box on this!

◉ When taking up a challenge such as this, you may need to take one or two different approaches. If you don't get it right the first time, keep starting from a different point until it works.

Natural talent

Mother nature is often the best designer and has provided inspiration for some important inventions. See if you can match the invention on the left with the inspiration on the right.

1. Shinkansen bullet train
2. Futuristic car
3. Swimsuit
4. Self-cleaning paint
5. Road reflectors

A. Shark's skin
B. Lotus leaf
C. Cat's eyes
D. Trunkfish
E. Kingfisher's beak

◉ The field of science referred to above is known as biomimicry, which means "imitating nature." The next time you are in a park or garden, see if you can find inspiration or new ideas from the things you see around you.

Illustrated stories

Choose a painting—from an art book or from the Internet! Study the picture for a while and focus on the details. Let your mind wander and then try to create a story around it.

◉ Being able to understand and interpret artwork is a good creative exercise, as the brain thinks about what the artwork is showing and draws on what it means. By basing your story on something that inspires you, you may create something impressive yourself.

Back to basics

What can you do with an empty cardboard box? Use your imaginati and see if you can design somethin brilliant. Of course, you could alwa just copy our idea, but where's th fun in that?

◉ Some of the greatest inventors have taken simple things and used them in a new way. You don't always need elaborate materials to come up with great ideas!

ARE YOU A CREATIVE SPARK?

Lateral thinking

See if you can solve these riddles with a dash of imagination and a lot of lateral thinking.

Riddle A: Romeo and Juliet are lying dead on the floor. There are no marks on either of them, but they are soaked with water, and near them is a broken glass bowl. How did they die?

Riddle B: How do you throw a ball and make it come back without throwing the ball against a wall, the ball being attached to string or elastic, or the ball being caught and thrown back by someone?

Riddle C: A man rode into town on Wednesday. He stayed for three nights and then left on Wednesday. How is this possible?

When presented with riddles, we may try to find the answer based on a straightforward reading of the question. By trying to think what else the riddle might mean, you will learn to think laterally.

Something from nothing

There is great creative potential in the bits and pieces lying around your home. Try to find new ways to use everyday objects such as tissue boxes, cardboard tubes, and straws. Or maybe make a sculpture, starting with an empty egg carton and adding anything else that sparks your imagination.

You may come up with a fantastic creation, but even if your ideas turn out to be more silly than splendid, you will have learned a great deal about using your own creative spark.

Put your potential for brilliance to the test with these six challenges. Some of the games require lateral thinking, while others leave the creativity entirely in your hands. Just check the challenge in each cloud and see whether you qualify as a creative spark! You'll find the answers on page 189.

BUOST YUUR CREATIVITY

Many techniques designed to improve creative thinking encourage you to break away from strict logic and fixed ideas and let your mind wander more freely around a problem. This is often called "thinking outside the box." It helps you see things from different angles and come up with the fresh approaches you need to be creative.

Brainstorming

This involves thinking up as many ideas as possible without judging them. You can do this alone, but it is usually a group activity, with someone writing all the ideas down. It can be fun! When everyone has run out of ideas, you look at the list and see what you have. Sometimes the oddball ideas turn out to be the best ones.

Visual thinking

Instead of making simple lists of ideas, you can turn them into a diagram. You start with a central problem, such as global warming, and add a series of spreading branches depicting all the related facts, figures, and ideas. This can work like a visual form of brainstorming, with new ideas leading to more radical, creative ones.

Lateral thinking

Similar to brainstorming, lateral thinking is all about approaching a problem from every possible angle. The basic idea is to identify the "normal" way of looking at a problem and avoid it. You use a random way of triggering new trains of thought, such as letting a book fall open, sticking a pin on the page, and seeing how the word it hits might relate to the problem. It sounds crazy, but it can be surprisingly effective.

What if...?

One way of moving beyond fixed ideas is to ask, "What if . . .?" You could ask, "What if all bus travel was free?" and this might lead to creative thinking about the way we get around and the role of cars. It could be a negative question, such as "What if no one collected our garbage?" You could then figure out ways of dealing with the problem. Or the question could be impractical in itself, such as "What if our pets could talk?" This might seem like a fantasy, but it could stimulate useful ideas about how we treat animals.

I WALK MY HUMANS TWICE A DAY.

I TRAINED MINE TO WALK THEMSELVES.

Energetic thinking

Many people find that they think more creatively about problems while they are walking, running, or working out. The exercise has to be repetitive, so it frees your mind to work on the problem.

Working backward

If you know what you want but don't know how to get to there, try working backward. It's like working back from a winning shot in basketball: to get C to score, A has to pass the ball to B and B to C. Mentally, it can suggest ideas that would not occur to you otherwise.

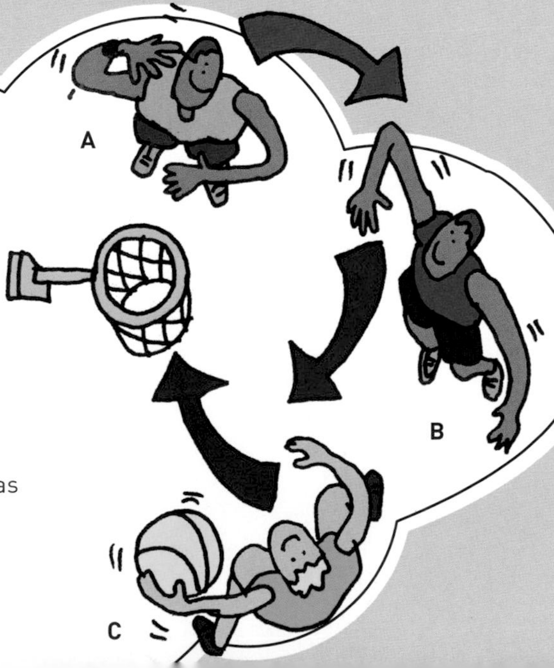

A

B

C

The technique of using diagrams to link ideas dates back to the 200s C.E., when it was used by philosopher Porphyry of Tyre.

You can improve your creative skills by following exercises designed to make you look at ideas and problems in different ways. So try these games and let your imagination run free!

Novel story
Use your imagination and think of ways of combining all the following words into a funny story or poem:

purple, sheep, chips, string, chair, summit, apple, screw, tie, smile

What if...?
Exercise your creative streak and come up with the most imaginative story you can to complete the following scenarios:

- What if we didn't sleep?
- What if your house could speak?
- What if we could go on vacation in space?
- What if our eyes were in our kneecaps?
- What if we could breathe underwater?

CREATIVE EXERCISES

Clip art
Can you think of 30 different ways of using a paper clip other than for holding papers together? Write down as many as you can in ten minutes. The crazier, the better. Ready, set, go!

Unusual crossing!
Imagine that you are stranded on one side of a lake, your friend is on the other, and you want to get to your friend. Set yourself a time limit of five minutes and write down as many ways you can think of to cross the lake. See what ideas your friends come up with, too. It could make for an interesting crossing!

Green credentials

Creativity is often about being aware of the world around us and using it for inspiration. When was the last time you really looked around you? Pick a color—for example, green. How many things can you see that are green? There are more than you might think at first.

Albert Einstein cultivated his own creative exercises. These "thought experiments" led to the development of his famous theories of relativity.

Creative play

Play helps free the mind and aid creativity, so use your visual imagination and plan a treasure hunt for your friends. Think of some cryptic clues to lead your friends on a journey around your house or backyard. The clues could even be pictures. Each clue leads to another until you reach the treasure. Read out the first clue and let the hunt begin!

Leonardo da Vinci

The *Mona Lisa* is thought to be a portrait of the wife of a wealthy silk merchant from Florence.

One of the most intelligent people ever to have lived, Leonardo da Vinci is famous for the amazing breadth of his interests. Primarily a painter of extraordinary skill, he became fascinated by the human body and pioneered the science of anatomy. He also became a practical engineer and inventor, dreaming up all kinds of astonishing devices that were way ahead of their time.

Amazing artist

Leonardo was born near Florence, Italy, in 1452. When he was 15, his father sent him to work as an apprentice for the Florentine painter Andrea del Verrochio. He soon became a superbly realistic painter of human figures, partly because of his interest in anatomy. He worked very slowly, and during the late 1400s, he completed only six paintings in 17 years. His most famous painting is the *Mona Lisa*, probably painted in around 1505.

Visionary engineer

In 1482, Leonardo got a well-paid job with the duke of Milan by describing himself as a military engineer. Luckily he was much more talented than most engineers of the time. He was interested in water power and came up with many devices driven by water wheels. Later, he proposed a bridge across the Gulf of Istanbul, which would have been the longest single-span bridge in the world, but it was never built.

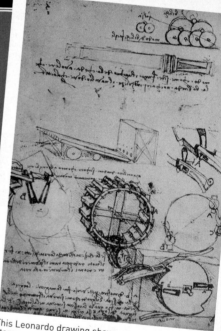

This Leonardo drawing shows a weapon for hurling stones—a bombard—powered by a water wheel.

Leonardo left most of his projects unfinished, and it is possible that he suffered from attention deficit disorder (ADD)—a psychological problem that has only recently been identified.

Ahead of his time

Many of Leonardo's inventions were objects that could not be made at the time but have since become a reality. He devised a form of parachute, a glider, a type of bicycle, a life jacket to keep a person afloat, an underwater breathing device, weapons that could be used to attack ships from underwater, and an "unsinkable" double-hulled ship. He even came up with this pioneering concept for a helicopter (left).

Today, Leonardo's paintings—and even his drawings—are among the most valuable in the world.

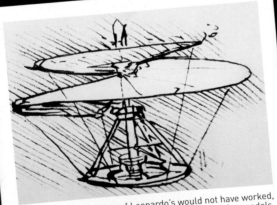

This helicopter of Leonardo's would not have worked, although his notes suggest that he did build flying models.

Notes and sketches

We know about Leonardo's many talents because he kept notes illustrated with detailed sketches. An intriguing feature of these notes is that they are written from right to left in "mirror" writing. We know that Leonardo was left-handed, which makes writing left to right in ink quite difficult because your writing hand smudges the wet ink. He possibly decided to get around this by writing backward—evidence of his original, logical thinking.

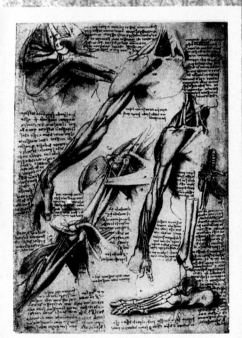

These studies of limbs by Leonardo were among the first anatomical drawings ever made.

Gruesome fascination

Leonardo was fascinated by human anatomy. He spent hours dissecting human corpses and drawing what he saw. This gruesome activity was considered suspicious, and was even forbidden by the pope himself, but Leonardo was not easily put off. He pressed on, producing many drawings, which he considered a much better way of describing anatomical features than written descriptions. Many of his drawings are remarkably detailed and accurate.

Scientific pioneer

Leonardo was interested in all forms of science, including optics, anatomy, zoology, botany, geology, and aerodynamics. More importantly, he pioneered a method of study that we still use today. Instead of getting information from classical authors and the Bible, he used the revolutionary approach of observing nature and asking simple questions like "How do birds fly?"

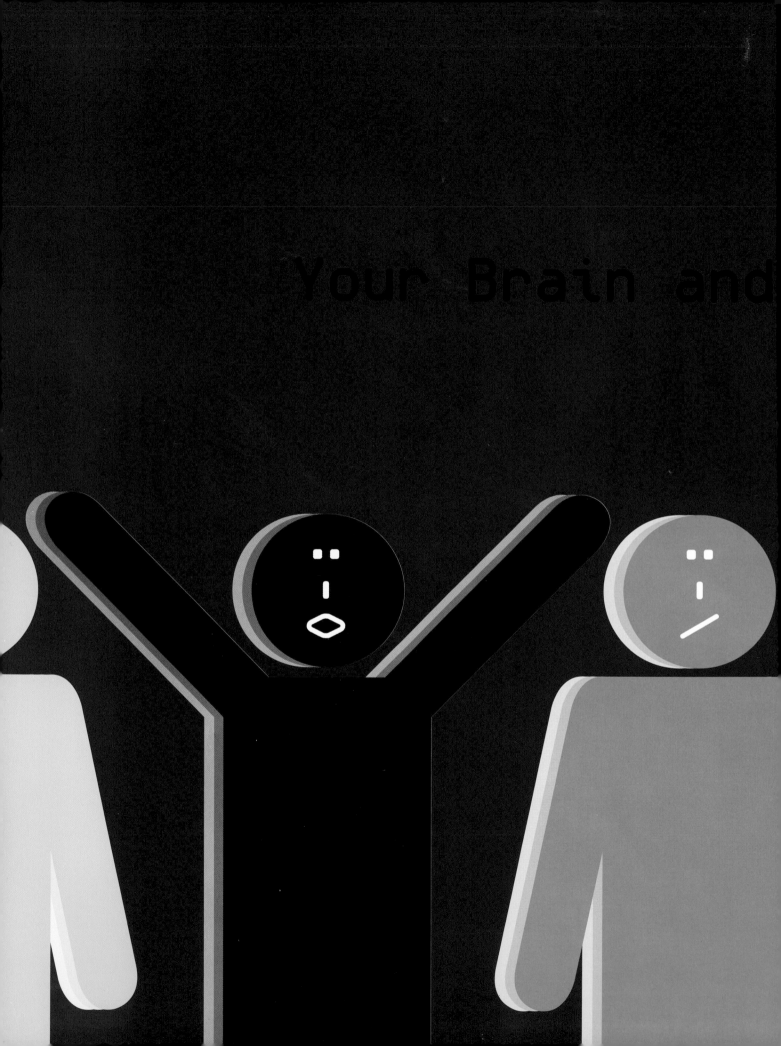

Your Brain and

SENSE OF SELF

You know who you are. You recognize yourself in mirrors and pictures. You have an image of yourself that includes your personality and your beliefs about how others see you. This self-awareness enables you to think about your identity and how you relate to other people. It is what we call consciousness.

The inner you
Most of us believe that we have an inner "self" that defines our personalities. The concept has no biological basis, and most scientists think it is an illusion. Yet it is a very powerful idea, and it forms the basis of the "soul" that many people believe survives even after death.

That's me!
If you put a cat in front of a mirror, it may not react at all. Birds don't recognize themselves either; instead, some see a rival and try to drive it away. Human babies are similar, but at the age of around 18 months, they know who they are looking at—they have developed a sense of self.

Self-esteem
We all have an idea of how we would like to be. If we think we don't match up to this ideal, we feel bad about ourselves—we have low self-esteem. Quite often the ideal is not realistic, but sometimes our judgment of our self is inaccurate and we are actually closer to the ideal than we think.

Brain HQ?

Scans of brain activity like this one, showing high activity in red, reveal that there isn't a single part of the brain that is the focus of consciousness. No one has ever suffered a brain injury that destroyed their sense of self but left everything else intact. Instead, it seems that consciousness depends on activity throughout the cerebral cortex—the part of the brain responsible for memory and thinking.

Some people suffer from a psychological condition that makes them think they have more than one "self." On average, they believe they have 13 different identities.

zzzzzzz

I look good, and I'm looking forward to seeing my friends later . . .

Self-image

Your sense of self is made up of your personal history combined with your own idea of your personality and physical appearance, as well as how others see you. If you are lucky, you will have a positive self-image, but some people have negative ideas that distort their self-image. For example, very shy people think others are judging them all the time.

Consciousness

No one really knows what consciousness is, but we all have it. It has been described as an awareness of our own existence and our thought processes. So it is partly about your identity but also about your ability to think, plan, and analyze your thoughts and plans.

PERSONALITY TYPES

Everyone is affected in different ways by the same experiences. Jack hates parties, but his friend Jill loves them. They have different personalities. Yet this might not predict how they react to other types of experiences. Jack might be open to new ideas, while Jill is not. We are all complex mixtures of a variety of personality traits.

The ancient Greeks thought there were only four basic personality types: happy, gloomy, calm, and excitable.

Getting along together
Some people are very reserved and have only a few special friends. Others are more sociable and seem to get along with everyone. Being open minded to the ideas of people with different personalities helps us develop both emotionally and intellectually. It also helps us cooperate to achieve things.

In the genes
Part of your personality is inherited from your parents, so if they are both fun-loving people, there's a good chance you will be the same. However, it is not quite so simple, because personality traits can be expressed in various ways. A well-organized artist, for example, might seem unlike a well-organized banker.

Individuality
Western cultures tend to celebrate the variations in personality that make us individuals. Some other cultures discourage them. However, we all seem to be getting bolder about our individuality, and we often display this in the way we dress and behave. Ideally, we would all feel confident as individuals while staying responsible members of society.

Nature and nurture
Your experiences can have a big effect on your personality. If your best friend is run over by a bus, for example, it affects your outlook. But although these twins may have been affected in different ways by their personal histories, they probably react to new experiences in similar ways.

Five-way split

Most psychologists agree that personality is defined by five traits, each with its own sliding scale. For each trait, every one of us lies at a different point on the scale. This gives a wide range of possible combinations and accounts for the almost infinite variety of human personalities.

Neuroticism

Worried
Insecure
Self-pitying

Calm
Secure
Self-satisfied

Extroversion

Sociable
Fun loving
Affectionate

Shy
Serious
Reserved

Openness

Imaginative
Independent
Prefers variety

Down-to-earth
Conforming
Prefers routine

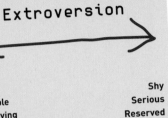

Agreeableness

Helpful
Softhearted
Trusting

Unhelpful
Ruthless
Suspicious

Simple systems

People often use simple ways of defining personality. One common system is the type A person who is dynamic and pushy—such as the girl in the above pictures—and the type B person who is more relaxed. But these simple concepts do not cover all aspects of personality.

Conscientiousness

Organized
Careful
Self disciplined

Disorganized
Careless
Weak willed

WHAT ABOUT YOU?

Personality test

For each questions, answer "yes," "no," or "not sure." There are no right or wrong answers—just choose the answer that you think best describes you and then follow the instructions below to add up your score and see what your results reveal.

Everyone is a mix of emotions, habits, and traits—put them all together and you get your own unique personality. But how well do you know yourself? Take this personality test and find out more.

1 Do you like doing things that are a bit dangerous?

2 Are you afraid to tell someone when you don't like them?

3 Do you enjoy having long phone conversations?

4 Are you good at remembering birthdays?

5 Would you rather hang out in a large group than with one or two good friends?

6 Are you very sensitive to criticism?

7 Do you get bored easily with new hobbies and keep starting new ones?

8 Do you enjoy meeting new people?

9 Do you usually do your homework on time?

10 Do you feel sorry for people

11 Do you usually manage to stay calm under pressure?

12 Would you usually "forgive and forget" when someone upsets you?

13 Do you think others would describe you as shy?

14 Do you usually have a plan for what you will do on weekends?

15 Do you make sure your room is neat and clean?

16 Do you rarely have arguments with other people?

17 Do you like exploring unfamiliar places?

18 Are you scared of what other people might think about you?

19 Do you ever offer to help with the laundry?

20 Do you consider yourself to be a rebel?

21 Do you usually do things to the

22 Would you like to try bungee jumping, skydiving, or white-water rafting?

23 Do you find that you often get angry about small things?

24 Does your music and fashion taste change often?

25 Do you trust people easily?

26 Do you enjoy any artistic or creative hobbies?

27 Would you speak up if you disagreed with someone?

28 Do you think you are carefree and relaxed?

29 When you start a book, do you usually finish it?

30 Do you feel anxious easily?

Personality types

Openness

If you are very open, you like to experience new things and you welcome change. You prefer spur-of-the-moment decisions to making plans, and you probably have a number of hobbies that you dip in and out of. If your score was low, you probably prefer to be in familiar surroundings and like routine. You may have one hobby that you are absorbed in.

Conscientiousness

A high score means that you are sensible, reliable, and hard working. People who are conscientious try to do their best in everything and are often very neat and organized. They can also be a little fussy. If your score was low, you may be a little disorganized and find finishing homework, or doing chores, very dull.

Extroversion

Extroverts love talking to people and are very confident. They crave excitement and fun and are often thrill seekers who like danger. The opposite of an extrovert is an introvert. Introverts prefer to be socialize with one or two good friends rather than a big group of people who they might not know. Introverts can often be shy.

Agreeableness

A high score means you are easy to get along with and very cooperative. If your score was low, perhaps you can be argumentative or too outspoken. Most people become more agreeable as they get older.

Neuroticism

If your score was high, you are likely to be emotionally sensitive and high strung. You might get worried, upset, or excited more easily than others do. A low score usually means you are a calm and relaxed type who rarely gets emotional.

Everyone has a little of each of the five personality types, but in varying amounts. You can be open as well as neurotic or a conscientious extrovert. Each of the five traits is independent from the others.

How to figure out your score

Openness: Score 2 points if you answered "yes" to questions 7, 17, 20, 24, and 26. Score 2 points if you answered "no" to question 14 and 1 point if you answered "not sure," to questions 11 or 28. Score 1 point if you answered "not sure," to questions 6, 11, 18, 23, 28, and 30.

Conscientiousness: Score 2 points if you answered "yes," and 1 point if you answered "not sure," to questions 4, 9, 15, 19, 21, and 29.

Agreeableness: Score 2 points if you answered "yes" to and 1 point if you answered "not sure," to questions 2, 10, 12, 16, 25, and 27.

Neuroticism: Score 2 points if you answered "yes" to questions 7, 14, 17, 20, 24, and 26.

Extroversion: Score 2 points if you answered "yes" to questions 1, 3, 5, 8, and 22. Score 2 points if you answered "no" to question 13. Score 1 point if you answered "not sure" to questions 1, 3, 5, 8, 13, and 22.

Add up your scores for each personality trait: 3 or less = low, 4–8 = medium, and 9 or more = high. Now read about the different personality traits—the higher your score for each one, the better it should describe you!

WHAT MAKES YOU TICK?

We all behave in different ways, and one important influence is the brain. Some psychologists believe that there are two main types of brains—male and female—each with different skills. Have you also noticed that some people are full of energy when others are thinking of going to bed? Why is this? Find out more about how your brain affects your behavior with these exercises.

Male or female brain?

Answer these quick questions and then turn to page 189 to find out whether you have male- or female-type skills.

1. When a friend is upset, do you feel upset, too?
2. Do you notice the big picture rather than the little details?
3. Do you pay attention to someone's body language when they're talking to you?
4. Are you happier when you are talking about people you know rather than about television and computer games?
5. Do you understand written information more easily than maps and diagrams?

turn to page 189

Check your fingers

Testosterone is the male sex hormone (a body chemical that causes changes in the body), but it is present in girls, too. If you had a high level of testosterone before you were born, your ring finger is usually longer than your index finger, and you're more likely to have a male brain.

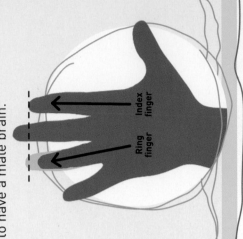

Index finger

Ring finger

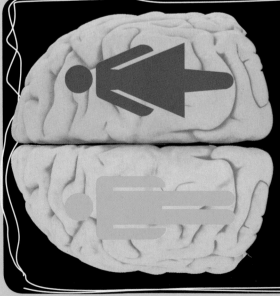

The bike test

People with predominantly male brains are better at noticing small details than those with female brains. A good way to demonstrate this is to ask a selection of friends, both male and female, to draw a bicycle from memory in 30 seconds. Compare their drawings. People with a male brain tend to draw bikes that are fairly close to the real thing, with a frame and saddle. Those with a female brain are more likely to draw something that could never work as a bike but may include a rider.

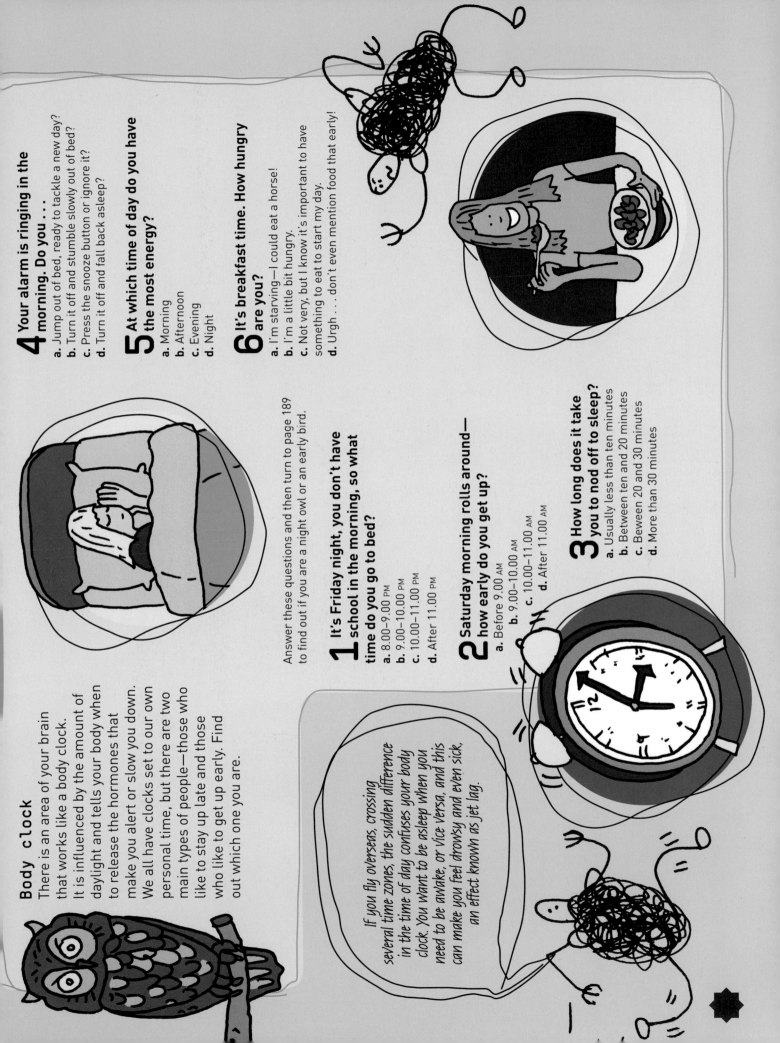

Body clock

There is an area of your brain that works like a body clock. It is influenced by the amount of daylight and tells your body when to release the hormones that make you alert or slow you down. We all have clocks set to our own personal time, but there are two main types of people—those who like to stay up late and those who like to get up early. Find out which one you are.

If you fly overseas, crossing several time zones, the sudden difference in the time of day confuses your body clock. You want to be asleep when you need to be awake, or vice versa, and this can make you feel drowsy and even sick, an effect known as jet lag.

Answer these questions and then turn to page 189 to find out if you are a night owl or an early bird.

1 It's Friday night, you don't have school in the morning, so what time do you go to bed?
a. 8.00–9.00 PM
b. 9.00–10.00 PM
c. 10.00–11.00 PM
d. After 11.00 PM

2 Saturday morning rolls around— how early do you get up?
a. Before 9.00 AM
b. 9.00–10.00 AM
c. 10.00–11.00 AM
d. After 11.00 AM

3 How long does it take you to nod off to sleep?
a. Usually less than ten minutes
b. Between ten and 20 minutes
c. Beween 20 and 30 minutes
d. More than 30 minutes

4 Your alarm is ringing in the morning. Do you . . .
a. Jump out of bed, ready to tackle a new day?
b. Turn it off and stumble slowly out of bed?
c. Press the snooze button or ignore it?
d. Turn it off and fall back asleep?

5 At which time of day do you have the most energy?
a. Morning
b. Afternoon
c. Evening
d. Night

6 It's breakfast time. How hungry are you?
a. I'm starving—I could eat a horse!
b. I'm a little bit hungry.
c. Not very, but I know it's important to have something to eat to start my day.
d. Urgh . . . don't even mention food that early!

Mary Anning

Born in England in the last year of the 1700s, Mary Anning was a self-taught pioneer of the new science of geology. She had a genius for finding the fossil remains of extinct animals and was considered an expert by some of the most eminent scientists in Europe. Yet she achieved all this at a time when women were barred from academic life.

An extinct relative of the modern nautilus, this ammonite is one of many fossils found on the Jurassic coast.

Jurassic coast

Mary lived in Lyme Regis on the "Jurassic coast" of southern England—so named because the cliffs contain fossils dating from the Jurassic period of the age of dinosaurs. In the early 1800s, such "curiosities" were not understood, but they were eagerly sought by visiting gentlemen naturalists. If they could not find any, they could buy them from local collectors like Mary.

This view shows Lyme Regis across the bay, and the beach in Charmouth where Mary found some of her best fossils.

Fossil hunter

Mary's father was a furniture maker and fossil collector who took his children fossil hunting along the shore. He sold his finds to wealthy visitors from a table in front of his store. But he died when Mary was 11, leaving his family with no income. His wife kept up the fossil trade, while Mary and her elder brother went out to look for fossils. Mary became an expert at finding, and identifying, exciting fossils, and when she was 20, she started to run the fossil business herself.

In 1800, at one year old, Mary survived being struck by lightning. People believed that this made her unusually bright and observant.

Marine reptiles

Mary made her first major discovery in 1811, after her brother found the fossilized skull of what he thought was a crocodile. It took her a whole year to uncover the complete skeleton of an ichthyosaur, a prehistoric marine reptile that resembled a dolphin. It was the first ever found. She sold the fossil to a rich local man, who sold it on to a museum in London. She was then only 12 years old.

Inspired by finds like Mary's, this old print shows what an ichthyosaur and a plesiosaur might have looked like.

Sea dragon

Wealthy collector Thomas Birch was so impressed by Mary's discoveries that he sold his own fossil collection in 1820 and gave the proceeds to the Annings. This established Mary in her business, and she went on to make other amazing finds. They included, in 1823, the first known skeleton of a long-necked "sea dragon," later described as a plesiosaur.

Mary on the shore of Lyme Regis with her geological hammer and Tray, her dog.

Renowned expert

Mary had little formal education, but she taught herself anatomy and geology. At an early age, she became lifelong friends with Henry de la Beche, who went on to become the president of the Geological Society of London. She knew many other eminent scientists, either personally or through letters, and by the mid-1820s, she was considered an expert on most types of fossils. Yet she rarely left Lyme Regis, and she visited London—then the center of the scientific world—only once.

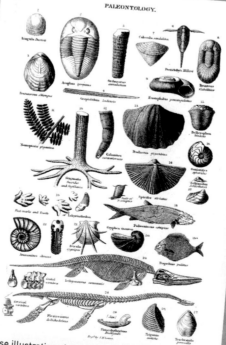

PALEONTOLOGY.

These illustrations from 1860 include an ichthyosaur and a plesiosaur, probably collected by Mary.

Geological pioneer

When Mary Anning was collecting fossils, most scientists still believed that Earth and its animals had been created in six days, only 6,000 years ago. The evolutionary theories of Charles Darwin were not published until 12 years after Mary died in 1847. Her fossils of extinct creatures were some of the most important geological discoveries of all time, and her ideas about what they meant forced scientists to look for different ways of explaining the history of life. In 1824, it was said of Mary, ". . . all acknowledge that she understands more of the science than anyone else in this kingdom."

THE UNCONSCIOUS

Only part of your life is controlled by the conscious part of your brain. A lot of mental activity is unconscious—or it is until you become aware of it. It includes primitive instincts and urges inherited from our distant ancestors but also your own perceptions and memories. These color your personality and affect your decisions, sometimes in strange ways.

> Some mental problems have an unconscious cause. If you become aware of the cause, the problem often goes away.

Perception

Scent is a powerful trigger of unconscious memories—the smell of grass reminds you of a day in the country, for example. Research has also shown that smells can influence behavior. People who eat in a room smelling faintly of cleaning products are much more likely to clean up after they have eaten than if the room has no scent.

Carl Jung

Swiss psychologist Carl Jung believed in the collective unconscious—a mass of buried memories inherited from our ancestors. He thought this explained the ghost stories, myths, and fairy tales that are part of every culture. However, since Jung's death in 1961, his theory has been displaced by other ideas.

Imagined illness

The unconscious mind can have a powerful influence on health. Some people suffer from psychosomatic illnesses—illnesses caused by mental problems, such as stress. On the other hand, people who are sick may recover after taking a "medicine" that they believe will cure them, even though it has no active ingredients. This is called the placebo effect.

Your unconscious mind can be difficult to control, but it is vital to your survival.

Instinct

Most of our unconscious mental activity seems to be guided by instinct. Brain scans of people tested for unconscious urges, such as greed, show activity in the primitive parts of the brain—the parts that we share with other animals. These areas control basic instincts such as appetite.

Advertising

Some advertising tries to influence the unconscious mind. It may use flashed messages, songs, or slogans or associations with everyday objects. For example, an advertisement for ice cream might be linked to a a catchy tune, making you think about buying ice cream whenever you hear it.

The part of the brain that controls strong emotions matures in your 20s.

Conscious control

People being tested for unconscious mental activity are never told what is going on, because this would make them control their reactions. Such conscious control enables people to overcome their unconscious urges, and this is an important element of civilization. If we followed our instincts without controlling them at all, society might fall apart.

Hidden meanings

The images that appear in dreams may be symbolic of something else. If you were to dream of being on a desert island, it might be because you want to escape from your normal life. This idea was once an important part of a therapy called psychoanalysis, but there is no evidence that dreams really work like this.

Links with reality

A dream often turns out to be your sleeping brain's explanation of something that is really happening. If a cat is yowling outside your bedroom window, you might dream about someone singing really badly! In one test, sleepers sprayed lightly with cold water said they dreamed of bathing, floods, or rain.

Scrambled events

Dreams usually link together a whole series of strange events. One minute you are riding through the house on a horse and the next minute you and the horse are having lunch. Your brain seems to have a large collection of images, which it uses to form a story. You realize how crazy the story is only when you wake up.

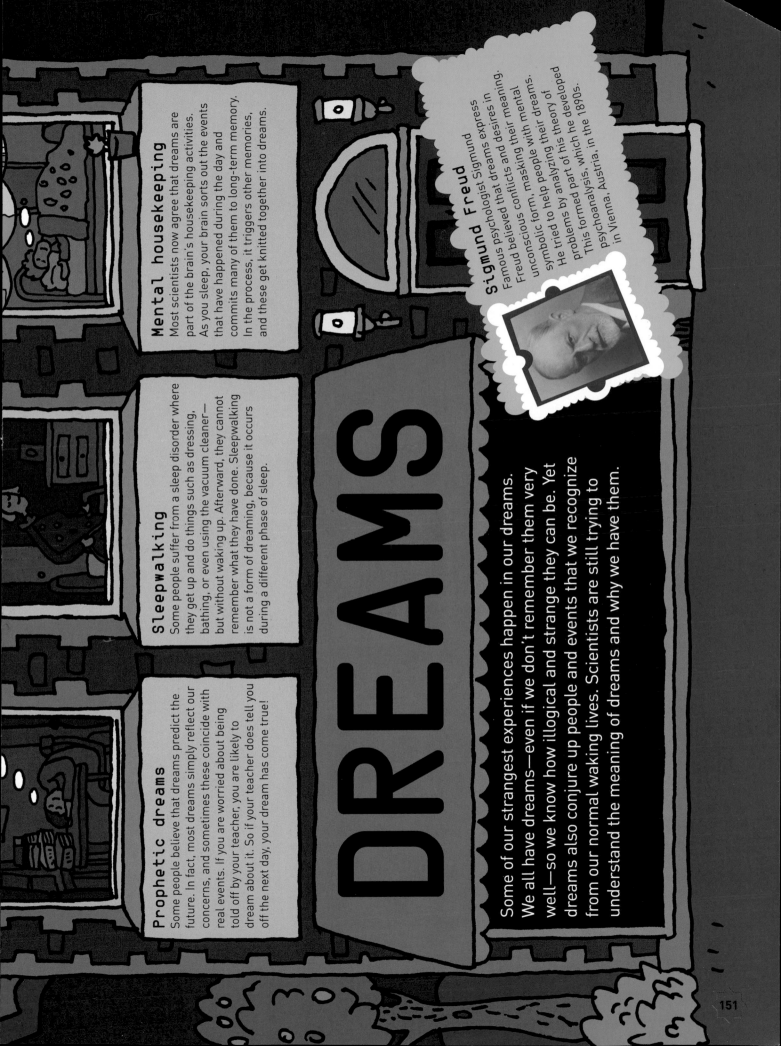

DREAMS

Some of our strangest experiences happen in our dreams. We all have dreams—even if we don't remember them very well—so we know how illogical and strange they can be. Yet dreams also conjure up people and events that we recognize from our normal waking lives. Scientists are still trying to understand the meaning of dreams and why we have them.

Mental housekeeping

Most scientists now agree that dreams are part of the brain's housekeeping activities. As you sleep, your brain sorts out the events that have happened during the day and commits many of them to long-term memory. In the process, it triggers other memories, and these get knitted together into dreams.

Sleepwalking

Some people suffer from a sleep disorder where they get up and do things such as dressing, bathing, or even using the vacuum cleaner—but without waking up. Afterward, they cannot remember what they have done. Sleepwalking is not a form of dreaming, because it occurs during a different phase of sleep.

Prophetic dreams

Some people believe that dreams predict the future. In fact, most dreams simply reflect our concerns, and sometimes these coincide with real events. If you are worried about being told off by your teacher, you are likely to dream about it. So if your teacher does tell you off the next day, your dream has come true!

Sigmund Freud

Famous psychologist Sigmund Freud believed that dreams express in unconscious form, masking with mental symbolic to help people their dreams. He tried by analyzing their of problems part of his developed This formed psychoanalysis, which he in the 1890s. in Vienna, Austria, in the 1890s.

EMOTIONS

We call intense feelings such as joy and fear our emotions. They seem to well up from deep inside the brain. This is because the most basic emotions are related to our primitive survival instincts. More complex emotions probably developed later in our evolutionary history. Our ability to control our emotions, and use them constructively, is sometimes described as emotional intelligence.

Emotion and mood
Feelings are powerful mental and physical experiences. The man above is enjoying a movie so much that he gets a surge of joy—he feels wonderful and can't stop smiling. Yet this intense feeling will not last long. It will be replaced by a calmer but more long-lasting mood of happiness.

Most women are more emotional than men, but this is partly because men are often expected to conceal their emotions.

Universal emotions
There are six main emotions, triggered from deep within the brain and beyond your conscious control. Your automatic reaction is shown by a facial expression that is the same whoever you are. The six people above are showing them all—fear, anger, and surprise in the front row, with joy, distress, and disgust in the row behind.

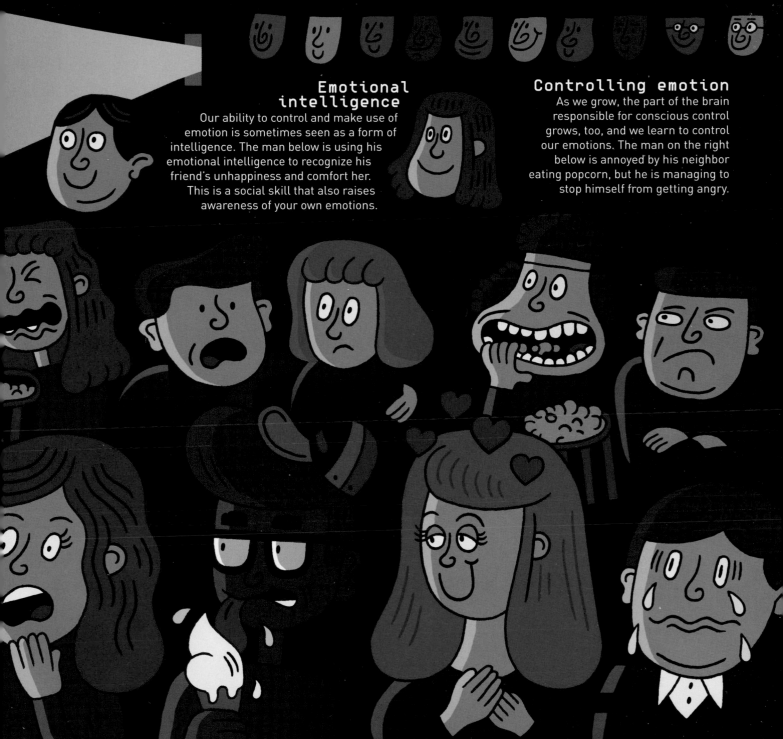

Emotional intelligence

Our ability to control and make use of emotion is sometimes seen as a form of intelligence. The man below is using his emotional intelligence to recognize his friend's unhappiness and comfort her. This is a social skill that also raises awareness of your own emotions.

Controlling emotion

As we grow, the part of the brain responsible for conscious control grows, too, and we learn to control our emotions. The man on the right below is annoyed by his neighbor eating popcorn, but he is managing to stop himself from getting angry.

Tears seem to wash away some natural chemicals that make you unhappy. This may be why you feel better after a "good cry."

Complex emotions

As well as the six basic emotions, we also experience up to 30 complex emotions such as guilt, irritation, alarm, pride, envy, and love. Many of these are related to the complexities of human society. They are less automatic, involving more thought—although emotions such as love can still seem difficult to control.

Crying

As far as we know, only humans cry. Crying in distress produces tears and a distinctive facial expression. Tears with a different expression can also be caused by joy, especially among adults. This may indicate that the mental wiring for distress and joy is connected.

Mahatma Gandhi

We do not often link politics with genius. Yet some political figures have the genius to see problems in a new way and use this insight to change history. One of the greatest was Mahatma Gandhi, the leader of the Indian independence movement. He pioneered resistance to authority by nonviolent mass civil disobedience—an idea that inspired movements for civil rights and freedom across the world.

Rude awakening

Born in 1869 in Gujarat, India, Mohandas Karamchand Gandhi studied to become a lawyer. In 1893, he went to work in South Africa on a 12-month contract and came face-to-face with racism when he was thrown off a train for refusing to give up his first-class seat. He became a political agitator, staying in South Africa to help resident Indians obtain the right to vote.

At the age of 19, Gandhi travelled to Great Britain to train as a lawyer at University College London.

In South Africa, Gandhi found racism in the courts, where he was not allowed to wear his turban.

Nonviolent protest

In 1906, the South African government tried to force resident Indians to carry registration cards. Gandhi called on Indians to defy the law but not use violence. During a seven-year campaign, thousands were jailed, beaten, or even shot— yet Gandhi stood firm. Eventually this harsh treatment of peaceful protesters forced the government to negotiate with Gandhi. Nonviolent protest had won its first victory.

Gandhi worked as a lawyer throughout his stay in South Africa. Here he is with his staff in 1903.

Great soul

Gandhi returned to British-ruled India in 1915 and became involved in the independence struggle. He campaigned against the unfair taxation of poor villagers, earning the name *Mahatma*, or "great soul." He always advocated nonviolent protest, even after the 1919 Amritsar Massacre in which British-commanded soldiers opened fire on an unarmed gathering, killing at least 379 people.

Spin doctor
In the 1920s, Gandhi continued to campaign for independence but also fought poverty and the caste system—the Hindu class system. He began to live a very simple life and chose to wear low-caste clothes instead of those associated with Western wealth. He urged all Indians to wear homespun cotton instead of cloth imported from Great Britain.

Gandhi spent part of every day spinning his own cloth and asked all Indians to do the same.

Gandhi (center, with stick) attracted thousands of followers during his "salt march" across India.

In 1930, Gandhi protested against the British-imposed salt tax by undertaking a 250-mile (400-km) "salt march" to the sea to make his own salt.

Powerful legacy
The origins of every nonviolent protest in modern times can be traced back to Gandhi. He was a major influence on the campaigns of civil-rights activists such as Martin Luther King, Jr. and Nelson Mandela. U.S. President Barack Obama said, "In my life, I have always looked to Mahatma Gandhi as an inspiration, because he embodies the kind of transformational change that can be made when ordinary people come together to do extraordinary things."

Martyr to the cause
In the early 1940s, Gandhi called on the British to "quit India." During the campaign, thousands of people were killed or injured by police gunfire, and many thousands more were arrested, including Gandhi himself. In 1947, independence was granted, but the country was split into Hindu India and Muslim Pakistan. Gandhi's opposition to this led to his assassination by a Hindu radical in 1948. Almost one million people attended his funeral.

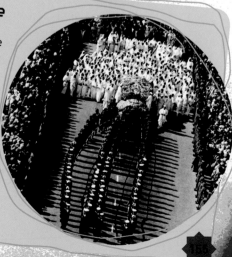

FEAR

When faced with dangerous situations, it is important to feel some level of fear. If you were not afraid of road traffic, for example, you might get knocked down by a car or truck. Fear triggers physical reactions that give you superpowers, so you can run away from a fierce dog and even jump over a fence to escape. However, many of the situations that frighten us in modern life do not require this type of physical response, and the fear can lead to stress-related illnesses.

The wiring of fear

When you are frightened, the thalamus, which processes sensory information, sends a nerve signal to a part of the brain called the amygdala. This alerts your adrenal glands to produce chemicals that prepare your body for action. Meanwhile, it sends another message to the prefrontal cortex of your brain so that you can analyze the threat.

Thalamus
Sends signal to amygdala

Prefrontal cortex

Amygdala
Triggers fear response

Supercharged

When the fear response is activated, your adrenal glands release chemicals such as adrenaline into your bloodstream. These chemicals combine with nerve signals to push up your breathing rate, increase the blood supply to your muscles, and intensify your awareness. You are briefly supercharged with the strength you need to survive.

Fight or flight

Fear is related to anger, and between the two they trigger the "fight or flight" response. This might give you the strength to wrestle a crocodile, but if you didn't have faith in your chances, it would also enable you to run away. The same response might also prompt you to rescue someone trapped in a burning building.

Wound up

Many of the events that frighten us in modern life cannot be easily resolved. Caught by his enemies, our hero is more worried about how his boss will react than anything else—and he cannot fight or run away from his boss. There is nothing he can do, so he just gets more upset. This type of stress can cause serious illness.

Working it off

When you get stressed, one way of dealing with the problem is to work it off with physical exercise. This uses up the chemicals that are supposed to help you fight or escape and makes you feel better. Exercise also encourages other parts of the brain to produce chemicals called endorphins that improve your state of mind and combat the effects of stress.

Relaxation

Many people use relaxation techniques to reduce the effects of fear-related stress. They include deep breathing exercises, meditation, and yoga. These can trigger a relaxation response, which works like an antidote to the fear response and helps you calm down.

READING EMOTIONS

You express emotions in ways that you are probably never aware of. It's not just what you say, but the way you say it, the look in your eyes, or the way you hold and move your body. A lot of this is beyond your conscious control. But we all try to conceal some emotions and even pretend to feel others. Sometimes this works, but often it doesn't, because your expression or body language doesn't quite match what you say.

We tend to trust people who do not conceal their emotions.

The six basic facial expressions of emotion are the same in all human cultures worldwide.

Facial expression
The basic facial expressions of emotion—joy, surprise, fear, anger, distress, and disgust—are easy to read. Some are even contagious: when you look at a smiling person, you usually start to smile yourself. Most of us can also recognize more subtle expressions such as doubt, guilt, or pride. The better you know someone, the easier it is to figure out.

Eye contact
We tend to read people's emotions by watching their eyes. In fact, it is not the eyes that express the emotion but the muscles around the eyes, which alter their shape. We cannot control this, which is why eye contact is so highly valued as a key to emotion. If someone keeps looking away, we may think that they are trying to conceal their emotions and deceive us— even though we are often mistaken.

A real smile looks different from a fake one because it is controlled by a different part of the brain.

Lie detection

Your emotions tend to trigger certain reactions if you are lying. Your heart rate and breathing speed up and you tend to sweat. These reactions can be monitored using electronic "lie detectors"—but good liars can stay calm and fool the system.

Body language

Our body postures say a lot about how we are feeling. Some are obvious, like jumping for joy or slumping in defeat. Many are harder to define and more difficult to pick up, but we can often read such body language anyway—especially when someone's expression doesn't match up. The confident body language but sad expression above gives a strange mixed message.

Faking it

We all try to conceal our emotions sometimes. We try not to look bored when visiting relatives or try to look happy when we are sad. Some people in public life make it their business to smile all the time. But the difference between a real smile and a fake one is obvious if you see them side by side—in a real smile, the eyes smile, too.

Acting

Actors are judged by their ability to express emotions that they do not really feel. This can be difficult, so one performance technique, known as "the Method," involves actors becoming immersed in the thoughts and emotions of the characters they are playing. Sometimes they do this so well that they get completely carried away.

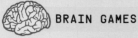

BODY TALK

It's not only your words that say a lot about you—your facial expressions and the way you move your body do, too. In fact, your body language often reveals a lot more than you want it to, because you don't realize what you are doing. Try these exercises and then check your answers on page 189 to see how good you are at reading emotions.

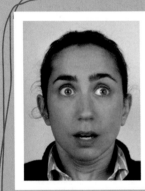 **A**

 **B**

 **C**

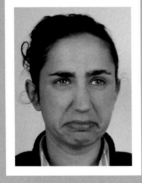 **D**

 **E**

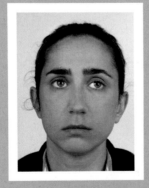 **F**

Figuring faces
Facial expressions often speak louder than words. Study the faces above and then see if you can match them to these six different emotions: anger, disgust, happiness, sadness, surprise, and contempt.

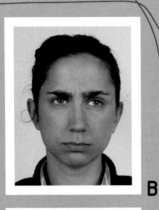 **A**

 **B**

Fake smiles
A real smile spreads across your whole face, while a fake smile is often mistimed, crooked, and leaves the eyes expressionless. Look at these six faces and see if you can sort the sham smiles from the genuine ones.

 **C**

 **D**

 **E**

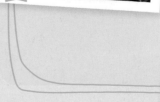  **F**

Psychologists believe we have around 7,000 different facial expressions.

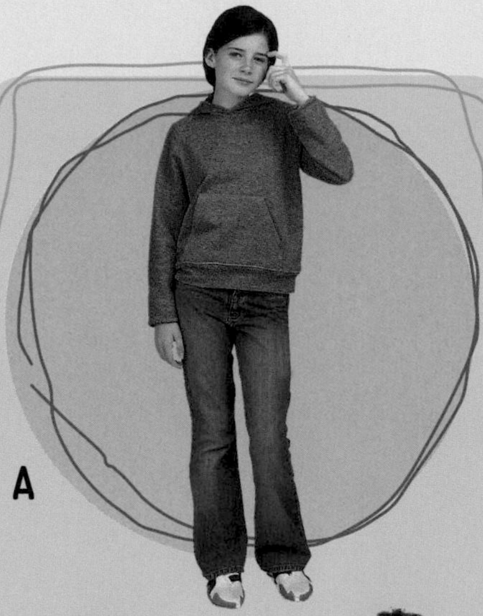

A

Certain types of body language can be interpreted differently by different cultures. Nodding your head means "yes" in most countries, but in Greece and Bulgaria, it means "no."

Body language

Some experts believe that body language accounts for 80 percent of communication. You may not be aware of it, but you do get a feeling that someone likes you, or not, without it ever being spoken about. Study these pictures and see if you can read the body language and match the poses with each of these messages: dominance, aggression, mimicking, submission, defensiveness, and dishonesty.

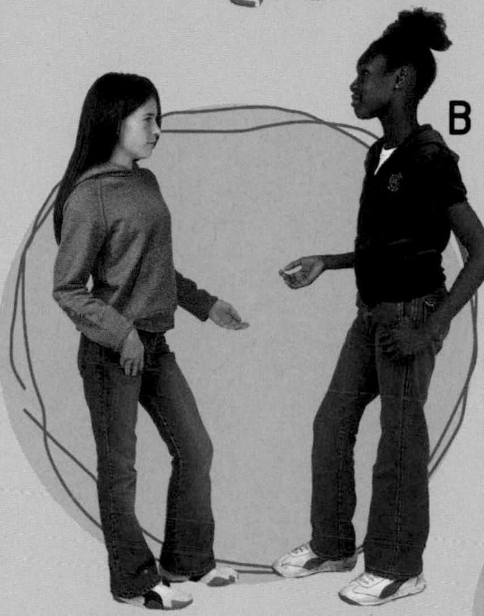

B

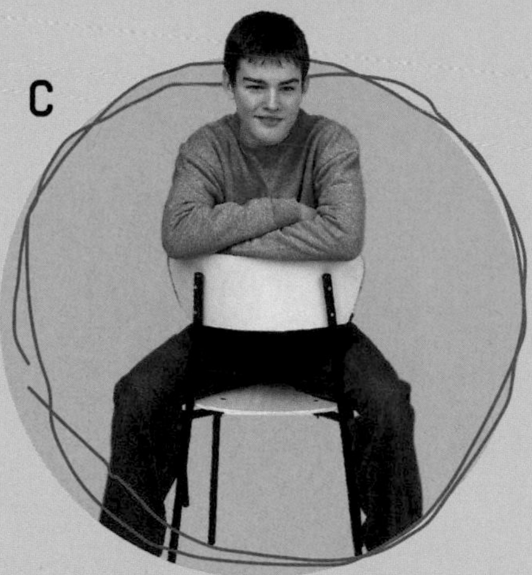

E

C

D

F

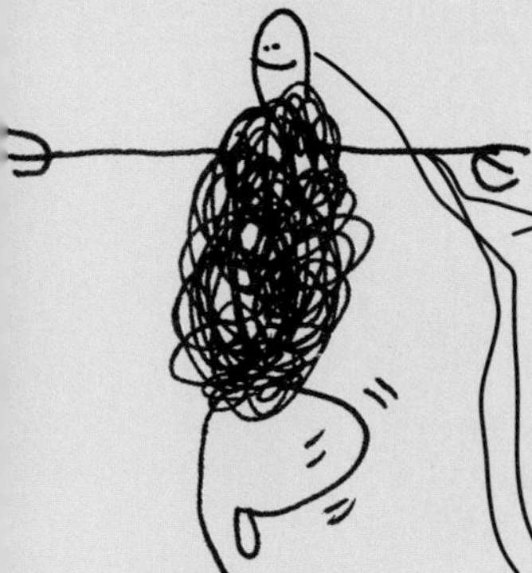

When someone is trying to control his or her facial expression, the true feeling, called a microexpression, usually shows on the person's face for a split second before being replaced with the one he or she is trying to show.

GOOD AND BAD
HABITS

We all have habits that help us get through life. When you wash your hands, do you stop to think how to get them wet, apply the soap, use it to clean your skin, and then rinse it off? Probably not. You automatically do it, because it's a habit. It's also useful, unlike bad habits such as nail biting. All habits are formed by repetition, which programs your brain so that you behave like a robot—and once formed, they can be very difficult to break.

Addiction
The most destructive habits are called addictions. The addictions that get in the news involve illegal drugs, alcohol, and tobacco, but people can also become addicted to things like sugary foods and chocolate. If they keep eating them, they can get sick, but despite this, they just can't stop—they are stuck with a bad habit.

Programmed behavior
Habits are formed by repeated patterns of behavior creating nerve networks in the brain. These work like the simple programs used in an appliance like a washing machine—once it is turned on, the program runs by itself. So when you start brushing your teeth, the habit program takes over to complete the job.

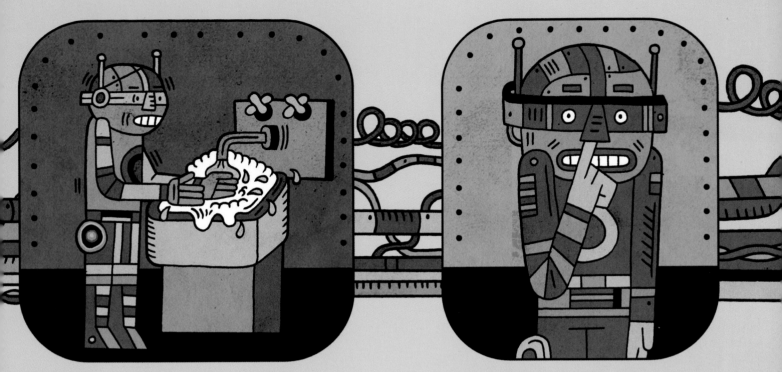

Useful routine

Every day you do things without thinking much about them, because they are part of your daily routine. If something like washing your face becomes a habit, it helps ensure that you do it even if you're thinking about something else. So habits are valuable when they make life easier and encourage you to do the things that you need to do, which you might otherwise forget.

Bad habits

Unfortunately, it's very easy to pick up bad habits. A lot of people bite their fingernails or pick their noses. They often do not know that they are doing it, because they are thinking about something else. Sometimes this doesn't matter much, although it can be irritating for others. But some bad habits can be very damaging.

Triggers and prompts

Most habits are triggered by external signals. When a driver sees a red light, it makes him or her perform a series of actions that stops the car. It is like an instinct. You can sometimes think up your own ways of prompting useful habits—putting your toothbrush somewhere obvious might prompt you to use it, for example.

Breaking a bad habit

A bad habit can be difficult to break because it is wired into your brain. Even if you manage to overcome a bad habit for several months, the wiring is still there, ready to be reactivated by the relevant trigger. Time may help, but often the best tactic is to replace a bad habit with a less damaging one.

WINNING AND LOSING

Most people who take up a sport are trying to win, but this means that someone has to lose. The difference is usually put down to fitness and ability, but when physical skills are evenly matched, the winner is often the competitor who has the right mental attitude. The same is probably true of life.

Confidence
Confidence is vital to winning, and this has been proved by research. In one study, 24 people had their arms strength tested before an arm-wrestling match. The researchers deceived the competitors into believing that the weaker participants were the stronger ones. In ten out of 12 contests, the weaker wrestlers won!

Setting goals
To get anywhere, you need to set yourself goals. But don't go for the long-term goal of being the champion—you need short-term personal targets that you can try to hit every day. If you are a cyclist, for example, your short-term goal could be to achieve a faster time than before—regardless of who wins the race. This will increase your confidence.

Visualization
Get in the right frame of mind by recalling the sensation of success. Imagine yourself accepting the prize for first place—it feels good, doesn't it? This feeling can help you win. Also, before the event, visualize yourself moving smoothly through the activity, and you are more likely do it perfectly when it matters.

Almost 80 percent of sports studies show that setting personal goals is one of the best ways of enhancing performance.

Focus

Losing your temper if you lose a point will not help you win the next one. In fact, it will throw off your concentration. You have to control your emotions and focus on the future. Use a mental routine to refocus when something goes wrong. Try conjuring up an image of a role model and ask yourself how he or she would react. Would your hero throw a temper tantrum?

Mind games

Some competitors try to win by putting their opponents off their stroke. They might boast that they are going to beat you or try to distract you by fiddling with their shoelaces. Don't fall for it. If someone tries to make you feel small, focus on your own successes, and if he or she tries to distract you, ignore the person.

Competing for life

Not everyone enjoys sports, but we all face challenges in life that can end in success or failure. They may even involve direct competition. Since we all want to succeed at whatever we do, the mental techniques in sports can be useful for both achieving personal goals and inspiring others.

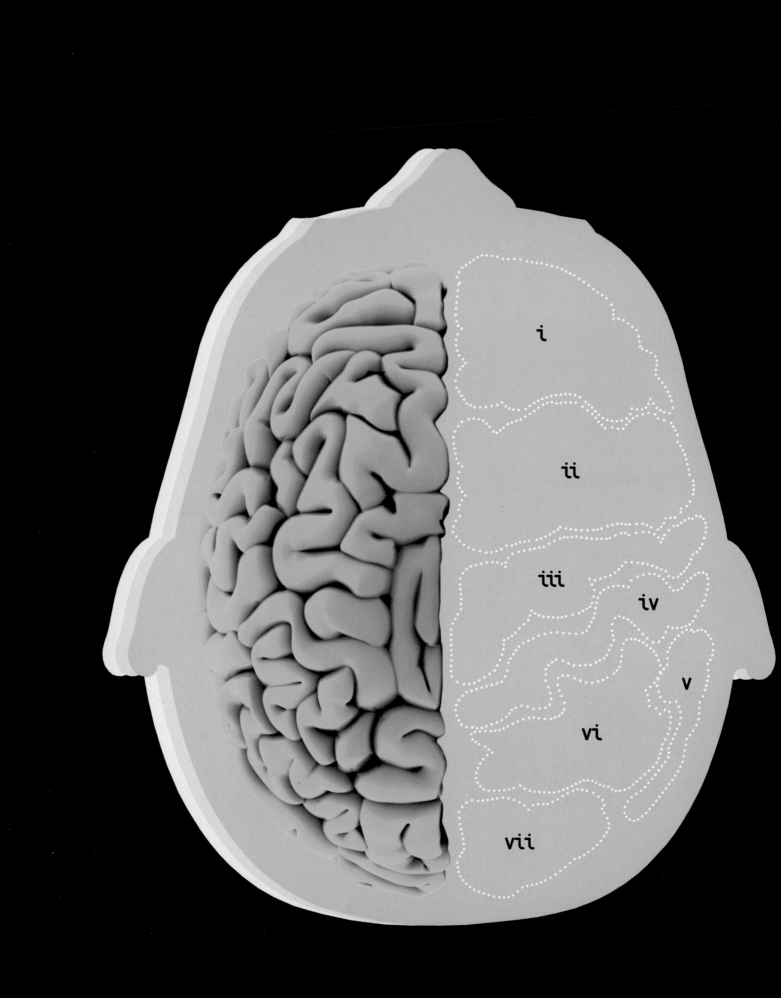

The Evolving Brain

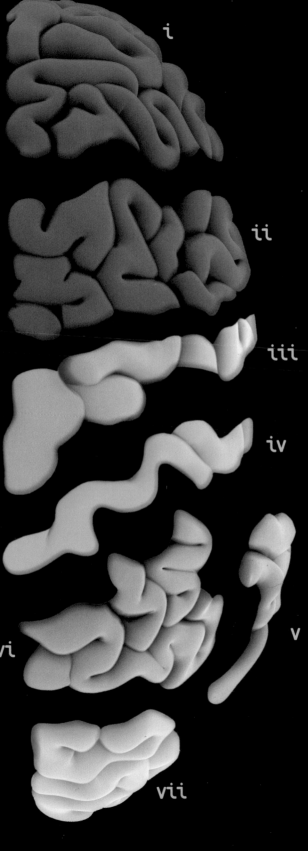

i

ii

iii

iv

v

vi

vii

HOW WE GOT OUR BRAINS

The most primitive animals do not have brains. A jellyfish has only a network of nerve fibers extending over its body, with no central control area to direct its actions. But most animals have brains of some kind to process sensory signals and enable them to respond to their surroundings. The part of the brain that does this processing has become hugely enlarged in the human brain. One part in particular—the prefrontal cortex—has expanded to give us our capacity for abstract thought.

Sensory tentacles
Gather information that must be processed by a brain of some kind, however primitive.

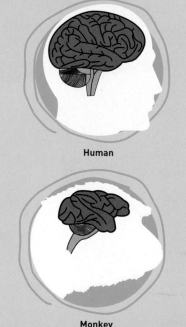

Human

Monkey

Heads and tails

Simple animals like jellyfish do not have brains because they have no heads or tails. The evolution of the brain began with the development of a "front end" to the body, because once an animal starts using only one end of itself to explore its world, its sense organs become grouped at that end. The sense organs need a nerve center to process their signals and send instructions to the rest of the body. So even a snail has a brain.

A large part of this owl's brain is dedicated to decoding the signals from its eyes and ears—making it an extremely efficient hunter.

Super senses

For most animals, the main job of the brain is to process data from the senses. This function is often more highly developed than it is in humans. A dog has a much greater ability than humans to identify scents, and some owls can use sound alone to pinpoint mice in total darkness. The brains of these animals have a lot of mental processing power, but compared to us, it is used in different ways.

Intellect central

The part of the brain that seems to be the main intellectual processing centre is the bulge at the front, behind your forehead—the prefrontal cortex. This uses information from the senses to form judgments, make choices, and predict future events. It has expanded in size throughout our evolution, pushing the human forehead forward compared to our monkeylike ancestors. However, a study of the brains of baboons—large monkeys—has shown that the human prefrontal cortex is not much bigger than theirs relative to the rest of the brain. So it is likely that its structure has also changed.

Instinct and thought

For a shark, the taste of blood in the water means only one thing—food! For a human, it could mean several things: "Have I cut myself? Is it someone else's blood? Where is the closest doctor? Will a shark detect it? Help!" The difference is that a shark doesn't give the blood much thought but acts on instinct. By contrast, humans tend to think about everything and may think so much that they suppress instincts that are crucial to survival.

Most of the behavior of this fearsome great white shark is driven by inherited instincts rather than conscious thoughts.

Human creativity took a great leap forward around 40,000 years ago, possibly because of improved language skills.

The first humans

Why and when did we get so intelligent? Our big brains probably evolved as our social nature gradually drove us to develop language. The ability to talk and plan became useful, so smart people were more successful and had more children. This process seems to have given rise to the first human species, Homo habilis, which evolved from a more primitive apelike ancestor around 2.3 million years ago.

Homo habilis
Known as Homo habilis, or "handy man," because they were the first to make stone tools.

These dancing or hunting figures were painted on the rocks of the northern Sahara Desert long before the land became a desert.

Intelligent ancestors

By 160,000 years ago, our own species—Homo sapiens—had evolved in Africa, and by 60,000 years ago, humans had spread across most of the globe. Compared to humans today, these people led primitive lives, but they needed to be smart to survive. Studies of their skulls show that their brains were probably just like ours, and they would have been just as capable of operating complex devices like computers if they had them. They have left evidence of their intelligence in the rock art that still survives in the places where they lived.

Charles Darwin

Darwin was only 23 when he embarked on the voyage that was to change his life and inspire his revolutionary theory.

English naturalist Charles Darwin revolutionized the way we see the living world. His theory of evolution by natural selection showed that competition for scarce resources led to species changing constantly through "the survival of the fittest." Published in 1859, the theory was a flash of genius backed up by a mass of evidence—the product of inspiration and a lot of hard work.

Distracted student

Born in England in 1809, Darwin went to the University of Cambridge to study for the church, but he was much more interested in studying nature. He became friends with John Stevens Henslow, a professor of botany, and Adam Sedgwick, one of the founders of modern geology. In 1831, he was on a geology field trip with Sedgwick when Henslow suggested that he join the survey ship HMS *Beagle* as "ship's naturalist" on an expedition to chart the coastline of South America.

When Darwin's great theory was published, his friend T. H. Huxley said, "How extremely stupid of me not to have thought of that!"

The *Beagle* was a small, cramped ship that had to be virtually rebuilt to survive the roughest seas on Earth.

The Beagle voyage

The voyage lasted five years, and while the crew charted the coastal waters, Darwin spent most of his time on land. He explored South America, where he found fossils of giant extinct animals. He visited the Galápagos Islands, where he saw that the animals on neighboring islands were similar but slightly different. He wondered if they might have changed over time—or evolved.

These Hawaiian honeycreepers all evolved from the same ancestor through natural selection.

Natural selection

Within one year of his return in 1836, Darwin was thinking about how animals might evolve. He realized that if food is difficult to find, animals that are less well equipped to find it tend to starve, while more favored animals flourish. Since all animals are slightly different from their parents, some are born with advantages that help them survive in particular environments. This leads to the evolution of species by a process that Dar...

When The Origin of Species went on sale, the entire first printing sold out on the first day.

Publication

Darwin realized that his theory denied the literal truth of the Bible, that God had created all species on Earth, so he did not dare publish his theory until he had gathered a mass of evidence to back it up. The process took him more than 20 years. But in 1858, he received a letter from another naturalist, Alfred Russel Wallace, that outlined the same theory. This forced him to prepare a shortened version of the book he was working on. Published in 1859, it was called *On the Origin of Species by Means of Natural Selection*.

The debate over the origins of humanity inspired many cartoons ridiculing Darwin.

Apes and angels

As Darwin feared, *The Origin of Species* caused a storm of controversy because it did not agree with the Bible. It also implied—without exactly saying so—that humanity had evolved from apes. Some people could not bear this idea and asked, "Are we descended from apes or angels?" However, Darwin's evidence was so good that his arguments could not be faulted on logical grounds.

Legacy

Most scientists now accept that Darwin's theory explains the mechanism behind evolution. It has also deprived the idea that the living world is unchanging and shown how fragile it can be. This has made us more aware of our impact on the environment that make up our planet so that we could preserve the never studied. Darwin suffered ill health and the completed publishing the died 73.

HOW THE BRAIN GROWS

Most of the development of the brain takes place before a baby is born, so at birth the brain contains almost all the nerve cells that it will ever have. During childhood, these cells are rearranged into increasingly complex networks that allow us to learn and remember. The brain reaches peak weight in early adulthood and then starts to shrink.

Making connections

During the months after birth, the brain develops fast. At first it has a simple cell structure that can control only the basic survival functions. But every new stimulus to the senses triggers the restructuring of nerve cells into the networks that store information and enable us to think. Like the girders below, they are rearranged into a new, more complex form.

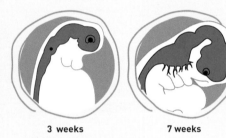

| 3 weeks | 7 weeks | 11 weeks |

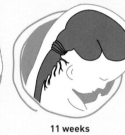

Beginnings

During the early stages of a baby's development in the womb, the brain forms at the end of a tube of cells that eventually becomes the spinal cord. At first it resembles the brain of a fish, with all the "primitive" parts well formed. But at around 11 weeks, the cerebrum starts to expand, until at birth it looks like a smaller version of a mature human brain.

Trimming down

Once the brain is up and running, it starts economizing on nerve cells. Inactivated cells are allowed to die off—a process that starts at the age of around four and continues for the rest of your life. This does not affect the brain's efficiency, however, because inactive brain cells have no function and simply waste energy. So they are thrown away, just like these spare girders being tossed into a Dumpster.

At times during the growth of an unborn baby, the brain develops at the rate of 250,000 nerve cells per minute.

Older and wiser?

As you get older, you definitely know more about the world and are able to make better decisions. But once you pass the age of 25, you often become less able to learn new skills that are not connected to the things you already know. This may reflect the fact that, in many people, the brain gradually loses weight, mostly through the loss of brain cells. But this mental decline is not an inevitable process.

Use it or lose it

There is plenty of evidence that intellectual challenges help slow down the decline of the brain during old age. People such as musicians, scientists, and political activists who keep working well past normal retirement age often show very few signs of mental aging until the last few months of life. Solving problems may seem like hard work, but it probably keeps your brain fit and healthy.

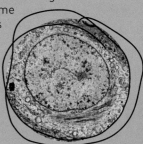

Nelson Mandela

Structural failure

Some unlucky people suffer brain damage in old age, or even younger. Some may suffer a stroke, which cuts off the blood supply to part of the brain, causing some of the brain tissue to die. Others may get Alzheimer's disease, which makes brain cells like these become tangled up and stop working, so sufferers can no longer think properly.

Damaged brain cell

SURGERY

Skulls showing signs of brain surgery have been found on European sites dated to around 7000 B.C.E.

The brain is the most delicate organ in the body, but it is also the least understood. When it suffers damage, either because of injury or disease, a surgeon attempting to repair the damage must avoid interfering with any healthy brain tissue, because the effects could be unpredictable and possibly disastrous. This makes brain surgery the most demanding of all medical skills.

Health risks

The brain is vulnerable to damage in a number of different ways. Physical trauma—a blow to the head—is common. Other problems include loss of blood supply to part of the brain (stroke), massive bleeding from an artery, and tumors or growths inside the brain. Brain surgery has also been used to deal with malfunctions such as epilepsy and Parkinson's disease.

Diagnosis

Identifying problems in the brain has been greatly simplified by brain scans like these. Not only can they locate the site of a problem, but they can also show nearby arteries and other vitally important structures, so the surgeon can plan the operation in advance.

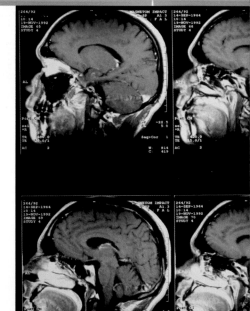

Brain surgery that once took 12 hours can now be completed in one or two hours, with better results.

Surgical precision

Thanks to three-dimensional computer-aided guidance systems, brain surgeons can reach damaged areas without harming nearby tissues. They can operate precisely with the aid of remote-controlled microscopes—shown in use here—and fiber-optic lighting.

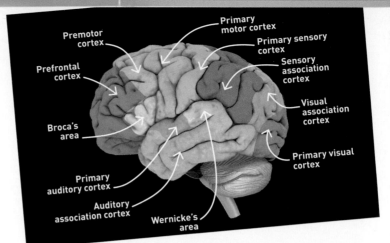

Premotor cortex · Primary motor cortex · Primary sensory cortex · Prefrontal cortex · Sensory association cortex · Broca's area · Visual association cortex · Primary visual cortex · Primary auditory cortex · Auditory association cortex · Wernicke's area

Discovery and learning

When a brain surgeon operates on a patient's brain, the area that is affected is precisely located and recorded. As a result, we now understand a lot more about the function of various parts of the brain, and this has increased the accuracy and effectiveness of brain surgery.

Radiotherapy

Some brain disease can be treated by therapies that don't involve cutting into the brain. They include radiotherapy, which uses a beam of radiation to destroy the cells that cause cancerous brain tumors. The beam is precisely targeted on the basis of a computer simulation, as seen here (right). It is painless but has to be repeated several times.

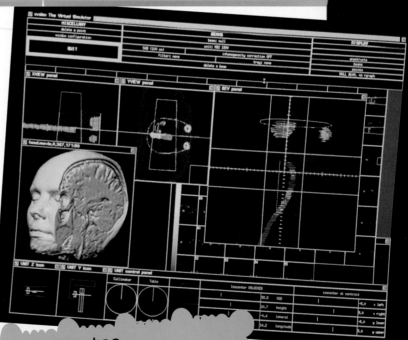

Hippocrates

Ancient Greek physician Hippocrates, who lived from around 460–370 B.C.E., wrote many texts on brain surgery. He described such as seizures and mental problems recognized the symptoms of spasms, recognized the symptoms of head injuries, and operated on patients with certain types of skull fractures.

ANIMAL
INTELLIGENCE

If you have a dog, you probably think it is intelligent. Sometimes it will do something that amazes you. But that is because we do not expect animals to think. We expect them to use the instincts that are programmed into their brains at birth rather than make use of the information in their memories to solve problems. But some animals do just that.

Trick and treat

Many stories of animal intelligence involve their devising ways of getting at food. Some people who put out food for garden birds, for example, find that it is often stolen by squirrels. The squirrels show amazing ingenuity as they overcome obstacles to break into "squirrel-proof" bird feeders. Hunger is a powerful motivator.

Toolmakers

Several animals are able to make and use tools—a skill that was once thought unique to humans. Chimpanzees, for example, use carefully selected straws and sticks to pick edible termites from their nests. If a stick is too thick to poke into the holes in a nest, a chimp will carefully peel back the bark until it is just the right size.

Crows are very bright birds. A crow offered a small food package in a glass tube is capable of picking up a piece of wire and bending it into a hook, which it uses to pull the food from the tube.

Some insects, such as termites, construct amazingly complex nests using instinct alone.

The most intelligent animals are vertebrates such as apes, dolphins, dogs, and crows, but intelligence is also highly developed among octopuses and their relatives.

Memory
There are many examples of animals with excellent memories. Some birds remember where they buried food stored for the winter, several months before. In Africa, crocodiles remember exactly when migrating antelope have to cross a certain river twice a year and gather there to ambush them.

Communication
Animals are also able to communicate. Dolphins have been able to learn a form of sign language that mimics spoken language and follow signed instructions to perform tricks that they had never tried before. A collie named Rico showed that he understood the names of 200 toys. He learned the words as quickly as a human toddler.

Smarter than us?
In some ways, animals are smarter than us. Migrating birds such as geese can accurately navigate over vast distances using the stars and Sun to guide them. During earthquakes and tsunamis, animals often seem to sense the impending disaster and take action, such as moving to higher ground to escape drowning.

Consciousness
It is difficult to say whether animals have a concept of "self." It is likely that some animals do have some idea of their identity, because this would explain the origin of human consciousness. So if you think your dog knows its own mind, you are probably right.

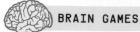
TRAIN YOUR PET

It's not just dogs that can be taught new tricks—many pets can be taught to do something. Even your goldfish can be coached to impress your friends if you train it. Here are some fun activities to try with all sorts of pets—but you must check with an adult before you start.

Ham-standing!

Hamsters can provide lots of entertainment, but they can easily get bored. This is a good way to spend lots of time with them, keep them active, and teach them a cool trick.

Step 1

Show your hamster a treat in your hand and then hold it above its head.

Step 2

Say, "Stand" until your hamster reaches up on two legs to get the treat and give it lots of praise once it does. If you repeat this often enough, your hamster will associate you saying "stand" with a treat and will rise up on command.

You can also do this with other commands. Try saying "paw" while holding a treat in front of your hamster—it will reach a paw to get it!

Young hamsters—around one or two months old—are the easiest to train.

New tricks for old dogs

If you have a dog, he or she may already know how to sit, stay, lie down, and beg. So here are two more tricks to add to the collection of skills.

Trick 1

Next time your dog yawns, ask him, "Are you sleepy?" Do this every time you catch him yawning and praise him as he does it. Eventually, he will yawn whenever you ask him if he is sleepy.

Trick 2

You can also teach your dog to walk or run around you in circles. Start by showing him a treat and then moving it around your body so that he follows it. Reward him with the treat and congratulate him.

It is possible to teach an old dog new tricks, but they may not learn as quickly as when they were young.

Take your guinea pig for a walk

Guinea pigs might not be as smart as dogs, but they are intelligent enough to be trained to walk on a leash. This gives you the chance to give your pet some exercise and to show it off to your friends.

Step 1

Start by getting a leash small enough for your guinea pig. Sit it on your lap with its favorite food and give it a lot of attention. While it is eating, slip the leash on, and let your pet get used to wearing it for a while.

Shake hands with your cat!

Just like humans, cats can be left- or right-pawed. They are also fiercely independent and are difficult to train as a result. With a little patience, this trick can work, especially if you start just before dinnertime!

Step 1
Have your cat's favorite treat in your hand and kneel down and show it to her, letting her smell it in your hand.

Step 2
Offer the hand that does not have the treat toward your cat, and hold it just above eye level. Your cat should instinctively put her paw in your hand, searching for the treat. Praise her and reward her with the treat from your other hand. Repeat until she puts her paw in your hand as soon as you hold it out.

Some cats just like to be difficult and might walk off in disgust. But keep trying!

Eating out of your hands

Contrary to popular belief, goldfish can actually be quite clever. They can learn to recognize their owners and, with a little patience, can even be fed by hand.

Step 1
Use water-soaked goldfish pellets and hold them over the surface of the water. Don't get too close or you will scare your goldfish away.

Step 2
When your fish starts to rise toward you, drop the food in. Keep doing this at the same time each day, and you will notice that your goldfish will rise higher and higher. Eventually, it will come right to the surface, and you should be able to put the food directly into its mouth.

This takes a lot of practice and patience, and you must do it every day to get your goldfish used to the idea.

Step 2
Do this a few times and then try walking around a small area of the yard with it—you may have to sit still and let it walk around you while your pet adjusts to its new surroundings. Over time, it will relax and you should be able to go on short walks with your guinea pig.

Your guinea pig may be a little afraid to walk outside, so it's probably best not to leave your house or yard.

Pet rats are very clean—and also extremely loving and intelligent. Because their eyesight is poor, they will learn to recognize their owner by smell.

CAN MACHINES
THINK?

Most of us use machines such as computers and calculators that seem to be able to do things better than we can. Many products such as cars are even made by robots. But can these machines think? Mostly they can't—they simply follow instructions that have been programmed into them by people who do the thinking for them. But we are finding ways of making computers and robots learn from their mistakes, and this is enabling some machines to display a form of intelligence.

Tireless robots

Many factories now use robots to work on production lines. They are controlled by computers that are programmed with all the instructions for the task. They work fast and they always do it right. The computers never forget anything vital and the robots never get tired. This makes them ideal for complex but repetitive jobs. But they only do what they are programmed to do, because they don't know how to do anything else, and they can't learn.

Computer power

If you program a computer or robot to play chess, it runs through hundreds of thousands of options before making each move. It does this in seconds, but it's inefficient compared to an intelligent human player who, with experience, will explore only the best moves. Yet it's not the robot's fault—it's the way it's been programmed. A better program might enable it to work more intelligently.

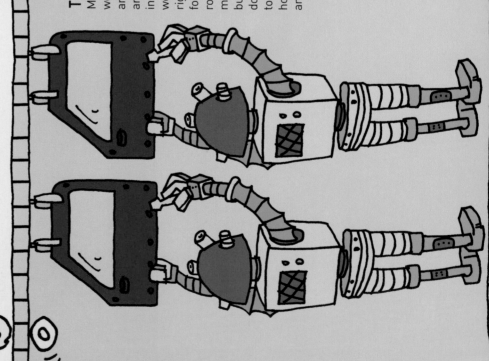

Artificial intelligence

When we learn, nerve cells in our brains are rewired into new networks. Engineers have found ways of making computer circuits automatically do the same thing in response to good or bad results. This means they can "learn" and display what is known as artificial intelligence.

Useful applications

Intelligent machines can do more than play chess or make cars. One really useful application is to make use of their excellent memories. Everything we know about a subject can be programmed into a machine, which can then be used as an electronic expert. This has already been tried for medical conditions. The machine processes all the facts about the patient's problem, figures out what it is, and comes up with the right treatment.

Understanding intelligence

Getting machines to act intelligently is proving very difficult and demands immense computing power—which just shows how complex our brains are. But part of the problem is that we do not really know how human intelligence works, and we cannot replicate something that we do not understand. We might be able to get simple computers to think intelligently if we only knew how to program them.

Thinking about thinking

One day a device with artificial intelligence might be able to find ways of programming itself to think more efficiently. This would then lead to even better programming and therefore even smarter thinking. We could end up in a world in which machines are much smarter than we are.

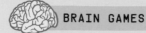

PROGRAM YOUR FRIEND

To perform even the simplest task, your brain weighs up a constant flow of information from your senses and effortlessly decides what to do. A machine, however, can only follow instructions. These games reveal how difficult it is to give and interpret instructions.

Puzzling time

A tangram is an ancient Chinese puzzle that can be arranged in many ways to make shapes. Your challenge here is to guide a friend to make pictures from these shapes.

You will need:
- Paper and scissors
- Ruler
- Colored pencils or pens
- A friend

Step 2

You are going to help your friend make a picture. However, he or she doesn't know what it is. Choose a picture from this page. Now give your friend precise one-step instructions as to how to arrange the pieces. For example, say, "Take the small brown square and place it on its point." This is surprisingly tricky.

Step 1

Using the tangram below as a guide, draw a square on a piece of paper and divide it into seven individual shapes. Then color and cut out each shape.

Step 3

Next it is your turn to make a picture based on the instructions of your friend. How does it feel to be the person receiving the instructions? How did you do compared to your friend?

Picture this

How good are your friends at giving clear instructions to achieve a common goal? Find out with this activity!

You will need:
- Paper
- Colored pencils or pens
- At least four friends
- Stopwatch

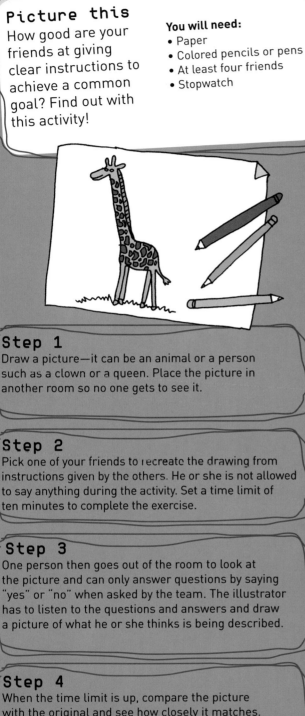

Step 1
Draw a picture—it can be an animal or a person such as a clown or a queen. Place the picture in another room so no one gets to see it.

Step 2
Pick one of your friends to recreate the drawing from instructions given by the others. He or she is not allowed to say anything during the activity. Set a time limit of ten minutes to complete the exercise.

Step 3
One person then goes out of the room to look at the picture and can only answer questions by saying "yes" or "no" when asked by the team. The illustrator has to listen to the questions and answers and draw a picture of what he or she thinks is being described.

Step 4
When the time limit is up, compare the picture with the original and see how closely it matches. If it doesn't, figure out where things went wrong so you will do better next time.

Play time!

Working in pairs, the object of this task is to direct your blindfolded partner to throw the ball and hit another blindfolded player using simple commands.

You will need:
- Several blindfolds
- Small foam ball
- At least six friends
- Stopwatch
- An adult to help judge

Step 1
Get into pairs and stand in a circle. One person in each pair must put on a blindfold. Set a time limit of ten minutes for the exercise. The game begins with one blindfolded player holding the ball.

Step 2
The players who are blindfolded are instructed by their partners how to throw the ball. For example, say, "Move to your right one step. Now throw." Or tell them when to duck so that they can defend themselves. When the ball lands near their partner, they must give clear instructions for retrieving the ball, such as "Bend down and reach out with your right hand."

Step 3
When the time limit is up, you can switch the blindfold to the other player and start again. Ask an adult to judge on how good you and your friends were at either listening or giving clear instructions.

GLOSSARY

anatomy
The study of the structure of living things.

association
The process by which new memories are linked to memories already stored in the brain.

atom
The smallest particle of a substance. Some substances such as oxygen contain only one type of atom, while others like water contain more than one type of atom.

attention
The first stage in committing something to memory by focusing on the moment or on the task at hand.

auditory
Having to do with hearing and sound.

axon
The long fiber that extends from a nerve cell, or neuron. Nerve signals pass down the axon in one direction, away from the main body of the cell, to stimulate other cells.

bacteria
Microscopic organisms with a simple single-celled structure. Some types of bacteria can cause disease.

botany
The study of plants.

brain stem
The region at the base of the brain where it joins the spinal cord.

Broca's area
The part of the brain that controls speech production.

cell
The smallest unit of a living thing. Many living things such as bacteria consist of only one cell, but the human body is made up of many cells, specialized for different jobs.

central nervous system
The brain and spinal cord.

cerebellum
A part of the brain that helps control balance and movement.

cerebral cortex
The entire wrinkly outer part of the brain that is responsible for sensory processing, memory, voluntary movement, and thinking.

cerebral hemisphere
One half of the cerebral cortex, or cerebrum.

cerebrum
Another name for the cerebral cortex, the cerebrum forms most of the human brain.

conditioning
A form of learning in which good or bad experiences create an automatic response to similar experiences.

conscious
Being mentally aware.

consciousness
A state of mental awareness.

dendrite
A short fiber extending from a nerve cell, or neuron, that picks up signals from other nerve cells.

evolution
The process by which things change slowly into different forms, usually applied to living things.

frontal lobe
The front part of each cerebral hemisphere, which plays an important role in thinking.

geology
The study of rocks.

hair cell
A cell equipped with a tiny flexible "hair" that is attached to nerves.

hormone
A substance released into the blood by a gland that effects change in another part of the body.

instinct
An automatic feeling or action.

intellectual
Anything to do with thinking.

intuition
Believing that you know something without knowing why. This is sometimes called a "sixth sense."

limbic system
A part of the brain that plays a role in automatic body functions, emotions, and the sense of smell.

logic
Sound reasoning that draws correct conclusions from basic facts.

mimicry
Copying the appearance or behavior of another person.

molecule
The smallest particle of a substance that can exist without breaking the substance into its component atoms. A single water molecule, for example, consists of two hydrogen atoms and one oxygen atom.

motor area
The region of the brain responsible for voluntary (controlled) movement of the body.

nerve
A bundle of fibers extending from nerve cells (neurons) that carries nerve signals, or impulses, between the brain and other parts of the body.

nerve cell
A specialized cell, also known as a neuron, that carries nerve signals from and to all parts of the body and forms networks in the brain.

nerve impulse
An electrical signal that passes along the fibers extending from nerve cells (neurons) and carries coded information to the brain or other organs.

neuron
A single nerve cell.

nucleus
The control center of a cell.

olfactory
Having to do with the sense of smell.

parallax
A visual effect that makes close objects appear to move more than distant objects when you move your head and eyes. It is important in the perception of distance.

parietal lobe
The part of the brain that interprets touch, pain, and temperature.

perception
The process of becoming aware of something through your senses.

peripheral nervous system
The outer network of small nerves that are connected to the muscles, skin, and all the organs besides the brain. It is linked to the central nervous system.

personality
The combination of character traits that makes you an individual.

perspective
A visual effect that makes parallel lines such as railroad tracks appear to converge with distance.

PET scan
A medical scanning technique using a system called positron emission tomography, often used to detect and locate activity in the brain.

philosophy
The study of the nature of knowledge.

phobia
A fear of something that has no rational basis.

placebo effect
A psychological response to medical treatment whereby the patient believes that his or her health has improved, even if the medicine they received was fake.

prefrontal cortex
The area of the brain that is most actively involved in thinking.

prejudice
A judgment that is made before examining the facts.

prodigy
Someone who displays great talents or abilities at an unusually early age.

program
A list of instructions that directs the operation of an electronic device such as a computer. The term is also used to describe the code that controls some biological functions.

psychology
The science of the mind.

recall
The process of consciously retrieving a memory from the brain.

receptor
A structure that responds to a stimulus such as touch, light, or temperature.

recognition
The process of identifying familiar knowledge when it is presented to you.

reflex
An automatic reaction by nerves that triggers movement—for example, in response to sharp pain.

retina
The sheet of light-sensitive cells at the back of the eye.

robot
A mechanical device that automatically performs a task under the control of a computer. Often used to describe a machine that resembles a human.

sensory
Having to do with the senses: sight, hearing, taste, smell, and touch.

somatic sensory cortex
The part of the brain that analyzes nerve signals from the skin, muscles, and joints.

spatial
Having to do with shape and space.

spectrum
The entire range of visible colors, as seen in a rainbow.

spinal cord
The main bundle of nerve fibers. It extends from the brain, down to the lower backbone.

stereotype
A fixed idea or image of something, often based on very little evidence.

telepathy
The ability to read the mind of another person, probably through experience and guesswork rather than true mental communication.

thalamus
The part of the brain near its base that acts as a relay station for information from all the senses except smell.

therapy
Any treatment designed to relieve physical or psychological illness.

3-D [three-dimensional]
The term used to describe objects that have volume, with the third dimension of depth as well as the two other dimensions of height and width.

unconscious
Having to do with mental activity that does not involve any thought.

Wernicke's area
The part of the brain that interprets sound and visual data, vital to understanding language.

ANSWERS

6–7 Your amazing brain
Do you remember?

1. The shower
2. Running, skiing, swimming, playing soccer
3. His lungs
4. Red
5. His cat
6. Fish
7. One
8. Cat, dog, fish, bird, snail, rabbit
9. Bacon and eggs frying
10. An injured finger

If you got more than six answers right, your memory is in great shape.

Perfect pair
Shapes A and F fit together to make the hexagon.

Feel lost?

66–67 Do you remember?
Recognition vs. recall

Step 1
1. Israel—Jerusalem
2. France—Paris
3. India—New Delhi
4. Russia—Moscow
5. Czech Republic—Prague
6. Germany —Berlin
7. Afghanistan—Kabul
8. Canada—Ottowa
9. Denmark—Copenhagen
10. Argentina—Buenos Aires

Step 2
1. Spain—Madrid
2. Ireland—Dublin
3. China—Beijing
4. Sweden—Stockholm
5. Iraq—Baghdad
6. Netherlands—Amsterdam
7. Japan—Tokyo
8. Italy—Rome
9. Egypt—Cairo
10. Greece—Athens

68–69 Paying attention
Spot the difference

Who's who?
Freddy is Tortoise B.

78–79 Mastering mazes
The one-hand rule

Right or left?

Trial and error

Amazing mazes

Over and under

80–81 Puzzling patterns

All alone
The one creature that doesn't appear twice is the wasp.

Thinking ahead
Each part of the sequence begins with two yellow cupcakes and ends with a purple cupcake, and the number of pink cupcakes in between increases by one each time. The yellow cupcakes at the beginning of the sequence are at numbers 1, 5, and 10—the difference between the numbers increases by one each time. This means the next yellow cupcakes starting a new sequence will be at 16, 23, 31, 40, 50, 61, 73, 86, and 100. So the 49th cupcake will be purple and the 100th cupcake will be yellow.

A face in the crowd

Spot the sequence
A blue, an orange, and a blue flower complete the sequence.

Missing pieces
The four missing puzzle pieces are J, K, G, and F.

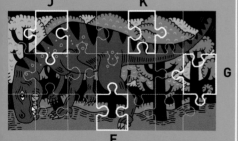

Perfect pairs

90–91 Brainteasers

Carnival money
The three boys initially paid $10 each, or $30. They are then given $3 back, which means they paid a total of $27 (the $25 entrance fee plus the $2 pocketed by the sales assistant). The $27 added to the $3 refund equals $30, so there's no missing money. In the puzzle, the $2 taken by the assistant is added to the $27 to create confusion.

The frustrated farmer
The farmer crosses first with the chicken and leaves it on the other side. He then returns, picks up the fox, and crosses again. Then he swaps the fox for the chicken so that they are not left together, and takes the chicken back. He then swaps the chicken for the grain and takes the grain across, leaving it with the fox. He then returns, picks up the chicken, and takes it to the other side.

Find the treat
She should choose Jar 2.

1. Lentils
2. Cookies
3. Flour
4. Beans
5. Pepper
6. Rice

Two at a time
Brother 1 and Brother 2 cross together, taking two minutes. Brother 1 returns, taking one minute. The father and grandfather cross together, taking ten minutes. Brother 2 returns, taking two minutes, then Brother 1 and Brother 2 cross together, taking two minutes.
2 + 1 + 10 + 2 + 2 = 17, so they should get to the train just in time.

The right door
The prisoner should ask each of the guards, "If I asked the other guard which is the door to freedom, what would he say?" If the door to freedom is the red one and he asked the guard who told the truth, the guard would say the blue door, because he would know the other guard would lie. If he asked the guard who always told lies, the guard would lie and say the blue door. Either way, the answer would be the same—they would both reveal the door with the lion behind it, and the prisoner should take the other door to freedom.

Who passed the package?
Stacey started the game.

92–93 Thinking inside the box

Tips and tricks

3	6	8	1	9	2	4	7	5
2	7	1	3	5	4	8	6	9
9	4	5	8	6	7	3	1	2
5	8	2	9	7	6	1	3	4
4	3	6	2	1	8	9	5	7
1	9	7	4	3	5	6	2	8
6	2	9	5	8	1	7	4	3
7	5	3	6	4	9	2	8	1
8	1	4	7	2	3	5	9	6

Starter Sudoku

1	7	6	4	2	8	3	5	9
2	5	4	9	3	1	7	8	6
8	3	9	5	7	6	1	2	4
7	2	5	3	8	4	6	9	1
6	1	3	2	5	9	4	7	8
4	9	8	1	6	7	2	3	5
5	4	1	7	9	2	8	6	3
9	8	7	6	1	3	5	4	2
3	6	2	8	4	5	9	1	7

Slightly harder

3	5	6	9	1	4	8	2	7
1	4	7	3	2	8	5	6	9
2	8	9	5	6	7	3	4	1
6	7	3	1	9	5	4	8	2
9	1	5	8	4	2	7	3	6
8	2	4	7	3	6	9	1	5
5	3	2	4	7	1	6	9	8
4	6	8	2	5	9	1	7	3
7	9	1	6	8	3	2	5	4

What to do

Now try this

Getting tricky

96–97 Think of a number

Puzzling pyramid

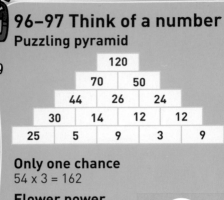

		120		
	70		50	
	44	26	24	
30		14	12	12
25	5	9	3	9

Only one chance
54 x 3 = 162

Flower power
Add the three largest numbers and then multiply them with the smallest.

5
7 **105** 6
8

The weighing game
Eleven strawberries balance one pineapple and three bananas.

Pineapple = 5 strawberries
Orange = 4 strawberries
Apple = 3 strawberries
Banana = 2 strawberries

Pieces of eight
888 + 88 + 8 + 8 + 8 = 1,000

Pass or fail?
Susan receives ten points for each of the correct questions, which gives her 150 points. But she got five wrong and five points are deducted for each, making a total of 25.

150 − 25 = 125

Susan has passed the test.

Dazzling stars

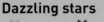

1   2   3   4

Multiple fractions
The answer is 5.

102–103 Seeing in 2-D

Up and down
Basket A will move up and Basket B will move down.

Five into four

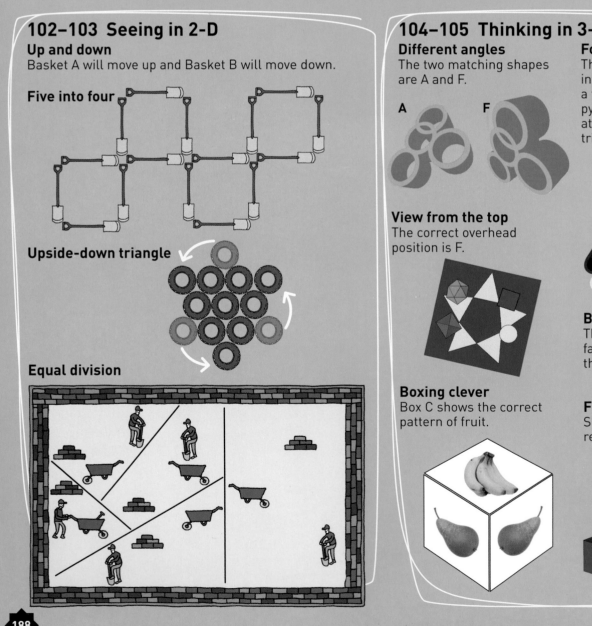

Upside-down triangle

Equal division

104–105 Thinking in 3-D

Different angles
The two matching shapes are A and F.

A   F

View from the top
The correct overhead position is F.

Boxing clever
Box C shows the correct pattern of fruit.

Four triangles
The pencils are moved into a 3-D shape called a tetrahedron (triangular pyramid) with a triangle at the base and three triangular sides.

Bottoms up
The color of the face-down side in the third picture is green.

Find the shape
Shape A shows the remaining pink section.

114–115 Having a word
Odd ones out
• **cat and cone**
The rest are boat related.
• **stapler and ruler**
You can't use them to write.
• **Moon and Sun**
All the rest are planets.
• **dolphin and sea horse**
They are not birds.
• **run and laugh**
The others are nouns.

Quick comparisons
• Bird is to beak as human is to mouth.
• Eyes are to sight as nose is to smell.
• In is to out as off is to on.
• Pen is to ink as brush is to paint.
• Tricycle is to three as bicycle is to two.

Like and unlike
LIKE
• hungry and starving
• tired and sleepy
• scary and spooky
• silly and foolish

UNLIKE
• praise and scorn
• edge and center
• rational and illogical
• leave and return

118–119 Words aloud
Fill in the blanks
hideous, tall, bloodcurdling, second, gripped, chance, shock, glimpse, surprise, flew

128–129 Are you a creative spark?
A dotty challenge

Natural talent
1—E The bullet train's unique nose-cone design was inspired by the beak of a kingfisher. The design enables the train to go faster, use less energy, and reduce noise levels.

2—D Mercedes-Benz has developed a concept car based on the angular body shape of the trunkfish. The shape makes the car spacious but lightweight, and it uses less fuel.

3—A Shark skin is made up of tiny toothlike scales that allow sharks to glide through the water. This feature has been used by swimsuit manufacturers to help competitive swimmers shave crucial seconds off their times.

4—B The surface structure of a lotus leaf stops water and dirt from building up on the plant. This has inspired a type of paint that is self-cleaning.

5—C After studying the way a cat's eyes reflected light, Percy Shaw developed his cats-eye road reflector in 1935. Today, cats-eye reflectors are used throughout the world.

Lateral thinking
Riddle A: Romeo and Juliet are goldfish. They died when their bowl fell and smashed to pieces.

Riddle B: Throw the ball straight up into the air.

Riddle C: The man's horse was named Wednesday.

144–145 What makes you tick?
Male or female brain?
If you answered "yes" to three or more questions, you have predominantly female brain skills. Female brains tend to be better at understanding emotions, feelings, and reading body language. Male brains generally have the advantage when it comes to understanding maps and technical matters and noticing detail. Girls can have male-type brains, and boys can have female-type brains, but most of us have a unique mixture of skills somewhere between the two types.

Body clock
Give yourself four points for each A, three for each B, two for each C, and one for each D.

6—11 points You're a night owl, who likes to stay up late, but make sure you don't miss out on sleep. Getting enough sleep is important—if you don't, you may be grumpy and your schoolwork may suffer.
12—18 points You're neither an owl, or an early bird, but have sensible sleeping habits.
19—24 points You're an early bird and wake up ready to seize the day—but try not to disturb the others!

160–161 Body talk
Figuring faces
A—surprise, **B**—anger, **C**—happiness, **D**—disgust, **E**—hatred, **F**—sadness

Sham smiles
Smiles A, C, and E are fake.

Body language
A—Dishonesty
People often fidget when they are lying, so watch out if someone rubs an eye, plays with their hands or feet, or pulls an ear.
B—Mimicking
When people get along really well, they often unconsciously copy each other's body language.
C—Dominance
A relaxed and focused posture often means that the person feels superior or powerful.
D—Aggression
A fight may be on the cards when two people face each other and stare while their bodies are tilted slightly away from each other.
E—Defensiveness
Closed postures are a good indication of defensiveness—look out for folded legs and arms, crossed ankles, and clenched hands.
F—Submission
Shy or embarrassed stances are common when someone is being submissive—people often look at the ground and sometimes hide their hands.

INDEX

Credits

DK would like to thank:

Niki Foreman, Karen Georghiou, Fran Jones, Ashwin Khurana, and Eleri Rankine for editorial assistance; Johnny Pau for design assistance; Stephanie Pliakas for Americanization; Jackie Brind for the index; Stefan Podhorodecki for photography; Steve Willis for retouching; Mark Longworth for additional illustrations; Tall Tree Ltd for design; Jaime Vives Piqueres for help with the POV programme.

The publisher would like to thank the following for their kind permission to reproduce their photographs:

Key: a-above; b-below/bottom; c-centre; f-far; l-left; r-right; t-top

akg-images: 108tl, 109tl; **Alamy Images:** Third Cross 59cla (carousel); Paul Doyle 64br; Richard Harding 58cb (spider); Interfoto 87tl, 122cla; Andre Jenny 85bc; Photos 12 148cl; **The Art Archive:** 122ftl; **The Bridgeman Art Library:** Bibliothèque de la Faculté de Médecine, Paris, France/ Archives Charmet 10bl; British Museum, London, UK 122cl; Massachusetts Historical Society, Boston, MA, USA 21cb; Musée des Beaux-Arts, Grenoble, France/Peter Willi 123clb; Natural History Museum, London, UK 171tl; **Corbis:** Alinari Archives 134cr; Bernard Annebicque 107clb; Arctic-Images 175cl; Artiga Photo/Flirt 140tr; Bettmann 21bl, 38bl, 39cr, 39tc, 73crb, 73tr, 84bl, 84crb, 84tl, 85 (background), 108bl, 135 (background), 135clb, 147tl, 154cr, 155c (background), 170c, 171bl, 175bc; Bettmann/Underwood & Underwood 21bl; George W. Ackerman/Bettmann 85tr; Adrian Burke 77crb; Chris Kleponis/Zuma 87tr;

Creasource 35br; DLILLC 95tr; Neville Elder 106br; EPA/Oliver Weiken 21fbr; EPA/MAST IRHAM 21crb (Venus & Serena); Randy Faris 62fbr; Rick Friedman 113bl (Chomsky); The Gallery Collection 38cr, 38tl, 122cr, 170tl; Gianni Dagli Orti 134bl, 134tl; Josh Gosfield 140bl; Waltraud Grubitzsch/epa 53bl; Historical Premium; Premium RM 151cra (Freud); Hulton-Deutsch Collection 19ca (Broca), 73 (background), 73ftl, 85cr, 109r; Jose Luis Pelaez, Inc 83br (boy); Brooks Kraft 13br; Latitude 61fcra (python); Philippe Lissac/GODONG 77br; Massimo Listri 120c; Yang Liu 56bc; Gideon Mendel 173crb; Ali Meyer 39 (background); Moodboard 140br; Dana Neely 174-175 (background); Michael Nicholson 171 (background); Norbert Wu/Science Faction 169tc; Historical Premium; Premium RM 151cra (Freud); Steve Prezant 140tl; Roger Ressmeyer 73tc; Ron Austing/Frank Lane Picture Agency 168c; Bob Rowan/ Progressive Image 76bl; Peet Simard 67cl; Tony Hallas/Science Faction 95ca; Frank Siteman/Science Faction 146tl; Dale C. Spartas 177br; Stapleton Collection 146c; Peter Turnley 112tc (signing); Randy M. Ury 69bl; Gregor Schuster/ zefa 174-175c (brain scans); M.Thomsen/Zefa 64cr; **DK Images: Geoff Brightling/Denoyer-Geppert 52bc;** Harry Taylor/Courtesy of the Natural History Museum, London 146bl; **Dreamstime. com:** 22cb (lemon), 22ftl, 23bc, 23cl, 74cl (pencil) 125ftl; Yuri Arcurs 58bc (dancing); Burning_liquid 59cla (beach); Creativeye99 59fcl (house); Davinci 125fcl; Derausdo 125cbl; Dimitrii 58cra (baby); Dndavis 58ca (keys); Dragoneye 125crb; Ejla 59bc (dog); Godfer 59clb (teens); Hansich

58tr (wedding cake); Kamchatka 58ca (cat); Kirza 125cr; Kmitu 59fcla (maths); Livingdedgrrl 59ftl (swimming); Moemrik 125cla; Monika3ste 125fclb; Mwproductions 58cla (class); Nikolais 124tr; Pemmett 125fcla; Prairierattler 59cla (net); Roim 124br; Scantynebula 58cl (teddy); Siloto 125ftr; Tass 59fbl (skier); Thijsone 125tc; trentham 125fcr; Trutta 125fcrb; Upimages 125bc; Uzuri 125cl; Winterling 124-125 (jigsaw); Zela 125ca; **© 2009 The M.C. Escher Company- Holland:** M.C. Escher's "Waterfall" © 2009 The M.C. Escher Company-Holland. All rights reserved. www. mcescher.com 32t; **FLPA:** Jan Van Arkel/ Minden Pictures 60bl, 60cb, 60l, 60tl; **Getty Images:** 109bl; American Images Inc. 97cl (apple), 97clb (apple); Blend Images 15tr; CGIBackgrounds.com 28cl; Ralph Crane/ Time & Life Pictures 108bc; Digital Vision 121fcr; Fox Photos/ 154bl; Henry Guttmann 154cla; Harry Sieplinga/HMS Images 44br; Haynes Archive/Popperfoto 155br; Gavin Hellier 122bl; Sandy Huffaker 52cl; Hulton Archive 20cr, 72br, 123bc; The Image Bank 119tr (glasses), 119tr (umbrella); Seth Joel 159tr; LWA/Dann Tardif 57tc; Mansell/Time & Life Pictures 147bc, 155tr; New Vision Technologies Inc 121cr; Thomas Northcut 119 (phone); Greg Pease/Photographer's Choice 29tl; Photographer's Choice 119ftr (bottle), 119tr (balloon); Popperfoto 155tl; Purestock 113c (student); Riser 119tr (cake); Yun Shouping/Bridgeman 121ca; Southern Stock 34cl; Stock Montage 20cl (Galileo); Pete Turner/Stone 29bl; Stone 119tr (coins); Taxi 119tr (earth); Tetra images 76cl; Mansell/Time & Life Pictures 20fcl (man); Time & Life Pictures 83tr (man), 123c; Guy Vanderelst 28br; John Woodcock

21fbl; Anna Yu 97tl; **iStockphoto.com:** 8-9ca (brain), 74-75 (gears),166l (brain); Marek Uliasz 20c; **www.kasparovagent.com, with kind permission of Garry Kasparov:** 21tr; **Lebrecht Music and Arts:** Ullstein-PWE 18cl (Hans Berger); **naturepl.com:** Andrew Cooper 60tr, 61bl; **NHPA/Photoshot:** Mike Lane 61cra (grass snake); **Photolibrary:** Big Cheese 56cl; **www.sandlotscience.com:** 'All is Vanity' Charles Allan Gilbert, 1873 - 1929 32b; **Science Photo Library:** 18-19bc (brain scan), 26cr, 27br, 27cl, 27tl, 72bl, 72fcl, 147 (Background), 147cl; Anatomical Travelogue 53cra; John Bavosi 11cr, 12-13cr; Martyn F. Chillmaid 45br; CNRI 106tr; Christian Darkin 87ca; Martin Dohrn 53cl; Emilio Segre Visual Archives/American Institute Of Physics 72tl; Eye Of Science 106c; Steve Gschmeissner 106fcl; Nancy Kedersha 17cr; Living Art Enterprises, Llc 53tc; Dr John Mazziotta Et Al 12bl; Will & Deni McIntyre 175crb; Hank Morgan 139tl; Sinclair Stammers 107bc; Thomas Deerinck, NCMIR 173fbr; **Still Pictures:** Ron Giling 120crb; **V&A Images, Victoria and Albert Museum:** 135tl; **Wellcome Library, London:** Dr Jonathan Clarke 16bl

Jacket images: Front: **DK Images:** NASA c (earth); Stephen Oliver cl (compass), cla (beaker); **Getty Images:** Photonica/A. T. White cr (hands); **Science Photo Library:** Pasieka cb; Tek Image cl (lightbulb)

All other images
© Dorling Kindersley
For further information see:
www.dkimages.com